Administrative Resource Manual

A Support Arm and Resource
Tool for Leaders

Administrative Resource Manual

Copyright © 1984, 1999
MESSENGER PUBLISHING HOUSE
Joplin, Missouri

No part of this book may be reproduced by any means without written permission from the publisher except for brief quotations used in scholarly publications.
Publishers Number 040104
ISBN 1-882449-23-1

Pentecostal Church of God
ADMINISTRATIVE RESOURCE MANUAL
A Support Arm and Resource Tool for Leaders

LEADER'S NAME

ADDRESS

TELEPHONE

- Pursuit of Excellence -

Contributors:
    James D. Gee, Editor in Chief
    Roy M. Chappell
    Ronald R. Minor
    Aaron M. Wilson

Published by
MESSENGER PUBLISHING HOUSE
Copyright 1984, 1999

Administrative Resource Manual

Table of Contents

SECTION ONE
Organization Orientation

Chapter 1 - Statement of Faith 7
Chapter 2 - Statement of Purpose 9
Chapter 3 - Definition/Orientation 13
Chapter 4 - Historical-Doctrinal-
    Governmental Statements 17
Chapter 5 - Organizational Structure 24
Chapter 6 - Affiliate Memberships 31

SECTION TWO
Program Administration

Chapter 7 - Program of Ministry 41
Chapter 8 - District Office Administration 47
Chapter 9 - Legal Documents
    /Technical Information 50
Chapter 10 - Planning and
    Conducting a District Convention 54
Chapter 11 - Mr. Chairman -
    Chairing the Business Session 70
Chapter 12 - Officiating at Ceremonies 73

SECTION THREE
Ministerial Credentials

Chapter 13 - Identification 89
Chapter 14 - Processing Credentials 92
Chapter 15 - Minister's Insurance Plan 125
Chapter 16 - Minister's Study Series 126
Chapter 17 - Applications and Related Forms 128

SECTION FOUR
Policy and Procedure

Chapter 18 - Policy/Procedure Explained 135
Chapter 19 - Planning Our Work,
Working Our Plan 140
Chapter 20 - Guide to Parliamentary Procedure 146

SECTION FIVE
Miscellaneous Information

Chapter 21 - District Accounting 194
Chapter 22 - Congregationalism and
the Pentecostal Church of God 200
Chapter 23 - Financial Support/Structure 206
Chapter 24 - Annual Church Report 212
Chapter 25 - Job (Position) Descriptions 216
Chapter 26 - Communications 226
Chapter 27 - Bits and Pieces 229
Chapter 28 - Bibliography 233

Administrative Resource Manual

- SECTION ONE -
ORGANIZATION & ORIENTATION

This section gives the Statement of Faith and Purpose, covers organizational and administrative orientation; identifies and communicates the historical, doctrinal and governmental philosophy; explains the structure of the organization so that the leader may be informed and able to communicate the same when called upon to do so.

A statement is a declared position that the constituency unites on and is loyal to. These stated positions are some elements we agree and promote throughout the Pentecostal Church of God.

Membership and leadership in any fellowship or organization demands loyalty of its constituents, which is proper if the organization is to achieve its purpose and objectives.

Chapter titles in Section One:
Chapter 1 - Statement of Faith
Chapter 2 - Statement of Purpose
Chapter 3 - Definition/Orientation
Chapter 4 - Historical-Doctrinal-
  Governmental Statement
Chapter 5 - Organizational Structure
Chapter 6 - Affiliate Membership

CHAPTER 1

Statement of Faith

WE BELIEVE . . .
1. In the verbal inspiration of the Scriptures, both the Old and New Testaments.
2. Our God is a trinity in unity, manifested in three persons: the Father, the Son, and the Holy Ghost.
3. In the Deity of our Lord Jesus Christ, in His virgin birth, in His sinless life, in His miracles, in His vicarious and atoning death on the cross, in His bodily resurrection, in His ascension to the right hand of the Father, and in His personal return to power and glory.
4. That regeneration by the Holy Ghost for the salvation of lost and sinful man, through faith in the shed blood of Jesus Christ, is absolutely essential.
5. In a life of holiness, without which no man can see the Lord, through sanctification as a definite, yet progressive, work of grace.
6. In the Baptism of the Holy Ghost, received subsequent to the new birth, with the speaking in

other tongues, as the Spirit gives utterance, as the initial physical sign and evidence.
7. In water baptism by immersion for believers only, which is a direct commandment of our Lord, in the Name of the Father, and of the Son and of the Holy Ghost.
8. In the Lord's supper and washing of the saints' feet.
9. That divine healing is provided for in the atonement and is available to all who truly believe.
10. In the pre-millennial second coming of Jesus: first, to resurrect the righteous dead and to catch away the living saints to meet Him in the air; and second, to reign on the earth a thousand years.
11. In the bodily resurrection of both the saved and the lost: they that are saved unto resurrection of life, and they that are lost unto the resurrection of damnation.

CHAPTER 2

Statement of Purpose

The purpose of the Church is to glorify God through worship, obedience to the Word of God and service. It is to edify the body of saints through nurture, cultivation and equipping for ministry. It is to evangelize the world by declaring the good news to all men.

Exaltation -   The Church existing for Christ
Edification -   The Church existing for itself
Evangelization - The Church existing for proclamation and action.

GENERAL CONSTITUTION AND BYLAWS
DEFINITION OF PURPOSE:

"As a Christian constituency of New Testament believers, we, the Pentecostal Church of God, subscribe to the following declaration of the things which are most surely believed among us (Luke 1:11), praying that there be no harmful nor divisive difference of belief to the injury of any, nor the disturbance of the peace and harmony of the Church, and that we may be all of the same mind and same judgment, speaking the same things in

Administrative Resource Manual

love (1 Corinthians 1:10; Acts 2:42) and with one voice glorifying God, to the edification of His people, and to give Christian witness to the world."

To define the purpose of the Church, we first look at the purpose of God concerning the Church. The purpose of God is to call out of the world a people who shall constitute the Body—the Church of Jesus Christ (Ecclesia). They are to assemble together for worship, fellowship and instruction in the Word of God. Being oriented to their stewardship and discipleship responsibility, equipped for service, God sends them back into the world as salt and light to witness and win the lost to Christ.

The Church can fail her mission either by being conformed to the world or withdrawn from the world.

According to the New Testament, the early Christians came together in such fellowship as a representative Body of blood-washed and Spirit-filled believers who cooperated with and sent out evangelists and missionaries. By leadership of the Holy Spirit, they set over the churches pastors, teachers and others to coordinate the work and lead in inspiration, instruction and involvement.

To achieve the purpose of the Church, vision and mission must be kept before the Body, otherwise we are lost on the sidelines and our prime time is given over to nonessentials and trivia. We must have proper perspective as to purpose (reason for existing; end result).

The Lord Himself determines the purpose of the Church. Our task is to clarify, communicate, and be committed to that purpose. We are to clarify Christ's purpose, as set forth in Scripture, to own it together and contend for it. An ultimate goal of the Christian's life is the upbuilding of the Church.

Statement of Purpose

Christ Himself molds the members of His Body together.

The gifts, abilities and capacities of one combined with others makes growth possible. "We are meant to hold firmly to the truth in love, and to grow up in every way into Christ the head. For it is from the head that the whole body, as a harmonious structure knit together by the joints with which it is provided, grows by the proper functioning of individual parts to its full maturity" (Ephesians 4:15,16, Phillips).

So then let us seek to glorify Him by worship, obedience to His Word and service.

In every way, let us support efforts to edify the Body of saints, equipping them for service. Let us be committed to world evangelization, thereby fulfilling our purpose and mission.

The General Administrative Offices coordinate the Church program and ministries nationally and internationally, and are a service center to all districts, fields, churches, ministers and members for the district programs and ministries.

The leadership purpose, on all levels, is to keep the vision before the people; to implement the purpose and inspire cooperation; to promote harmony of inter-relating parts which will result in achieving our God-given purpose, to manage resources necessary to accomplish the mission.

Purpose is like discipleship. You disciple one who in turn disciples another, and so on. When the purpose is owned by all members it sets in motion a multiplication process for growth. Every church effort should be geared to the three-fold purpose (exaltation, edification, evangelization). Let us proceed ON PURPOSE.

Administrative Resource Manual

The four-fold priority emphasis of the church should be, "purpose, people, program and property."

CHAPTER 3

Definition and Orientation

To familiarize ourselves with terms so as to better identify role specifications and environments, let us define the words to be used:

PURPOSE: "The object for which something is done; end in view; reason for being; an aim; the general reason for which the organization exists."

ORGANIZATION: "The systematic arrangement of relating parts."

ADMINISTRATION: "Working with and through people to get things done."

MANAGEMENT: "Meeting the needs of people as they work at accomplishing their goals."

ORIENTATION: "Familiarization with, and adaptation to, a situation or environment; awareness of one's environment; a period or process of introduction or adjustment."

STRUCTURE: "The arrangement or interrelating of all the parts as a whole—something composed of interrelating parts forming an organization." The specific form of organization used in any enterprise is dependent on local conditions, purposes and policies, available personnel, scale of

Administrative Resource Manual

operations, and diversity or simularity of services offered.

COORDINATION: "To bring into proper order or relation; adjustment of various parts so as to have harmonious action; to function harmoniously."

The leader's position in the movement is one of example and loyalty. The position of leadership is a giving and serving position. There is fulfillment and achievement in knowing that you please the Master and serve the Body.

Younger ministers often view leadership positions as glamorous roles of honor, not knowing the heavy responsibilities that go along with the position. It is a serving and giving role which should not make the position less desirable.

If we expect each minister to be a loyal member of the organization, how much more should we expect the leaders to be loyal.

Loyalty—"the state or quality of being faithful; faithfulness to engagement, to obligations." As leaders, we know that the organization is a means to an end and not an end in itself. It is a vehicle whereby we may fulfill our ministry and leadership to augment the ministry as a whole. We owe much to our movement for it has provided opportunities for growth, education and development, a place for our ministry and tools and materials for our work. We depend upon our leaders to inspire and motivate our people to the vision which we have shared and served faithfully since December 30, 1919.

As ministers and leaders we should adopt this attitude toward our church: "This is my church. I am a part of it. I will give my life's energies and talents to the work of God within this organization of which I am a member."

Definition and Orientation

Our future is as bright as the promises of God. With the cooperation of our leaders, we can experience the greatest days of growth ahead. TOGETHER WE . . . "Reach forth to that which is before us."

ADMINISTRATION DEFINITION AND FUNCTION:

Administration is the management and implementation of the program and purpose of our work. It is moving concept to reality.

A good administrator establishes the purpose, aims and objectives (or ends) of the organization he represents. He delegates and allocates authority and responsibilities. He must oversee the general implementation of the activities he has delegated (we succeed by what we inspect rather than from what we expect). In the New Testament, the word *kubernetes* (administration) is used three times. All three passages (Acts 27:11; Revelation 18:17; 1 Corinthians 12:28) indicate the idea of a helmsman steering the ship. Kenneth O. Gangel says it was the responsibility of this ship administrator to know the time of day, the nature and direction of storms, the habits of air currents, the process of steering by the stars and sun, and because of his knowledge, to correctly direct the ship. The helmsman is the responsible decision maker and has complete charge of the vessel's activity, in behalf of the owner. To guide the ship in the right direction, the administrator looks to the captain for his direction and orders. We as leaders today look to Christ as the Captain of our ship.

The word administrator is derived from the Latin word administrate, which literally means to serve or to minister. It has significance in our day as we

Administrative Resource Manual

evaluate what or whom we will serve. It's easy to stray from the main track of service to people and fragment our leadership. We need to rediscover our unique purpose and mission and build our ministries around them.

There are three primary purposes of administration: (1) to help the Church be the redemptive, covenant body Christ intended; (2) to enable the Church to be increasingly effective in carrying out its mission; and (3) to manage the affairs of the congregation as expeditiously as possible.

The three main elements of administration are the formulation of goals, the choice of ways and means, and the direction of people in some group purpose.

Administration is:

- The performance of a service in any capacity.
- The principles, practices and rationalized techniques employed in achieving the objectives or aims of an organization.
- The phase of business management which plans, organizes and controls the activities of an organization for the accomplishment of its objective in the long run and often is distinguished from operative management.

The administrator is a strategist: strategy is the planned use of all forces and resources available to an administrator in order to achieve an objective. As the wise man said, "Any enterprise is built by wise planning, becomes strong through common sense, and profits wonderfully by keeping abreast of the facts" (Proverbs 24:3, 4, LB).

CHAPTER 4
Historical - Doctrinal - Governmental Statements

Historically, the Pentecostal Church of God was formed December 30, 1919 in Chicago, Illinois by a group of ministers and laity who recognized that they could achieve through mutual strengths what they could not do individually.

The birth of our church took place during the great outpouring of the Holy Ghost at Topeka, Kansas and Azusa Street in Los Angeles. It was an humble beginning with principle roots of faith in the inerrancy and absolute authority of God's Word (from the Genesis account of creation to the final appeal in Revelation 22). This was the foundation upon which this new movement unswervingly stood and continues to stand.

The name of the organization in the beginning was the Pentecostal Assemblies of the U.S.A. However, on February 15, 1922, at the General Convention, the name was changed to Pentecostal Church of God and continues to be the same.

Through the years of development the Church has structured ministries in education through Sunday schools, Christian day schools and Bible colleges; missions through World Missions, Indian Missions, Home and Ethnic Missions; in ministries to the church such as the Pentecostal Young People's Association, the Women's Ministries, the King's Men Fellowship and the Senior Christian Fellowship and to the military through the Chaplaincy. Messenger Publishing House provides Sunday school curriculum, the Minister's Study Series, Bylaws, books, tracts, etc. The official publication for the church is *The Pentecostal Messenger*. We also publish a magazine called *Spirit* which is finding a special place of service for the local church. These publications greatly enhance the world ministry of the Church.

Through the years, God has given competent leadership to the movement on all levels: general, district and local. We are now located in 42 states, comprising 37 districts and four developing districts, with 1,243 churches. We have 3,109 churches in 48 foreign countries with a combined constituency of approximately 500,000.

Following our beginning in Chicago, Illinois, the General Headquarters was moved to Ottumwa, Iowa in 1927. Then in 1933, we moved to Kansas City, Missouri. Finally, in 1952, the General Headquarters was moved to Joplin, Missouri and remains at this location to date.

In the 1983 General Convention, it was decided to maintain our International Headquarters location in Joplin. After a survey was taken to consider moving to another city, it was agreed to purchase land and build new facilities for the General Administration Offices and Messenger Publishing House in Joplin, Missouri.

Historical - Doctrinal - Governmental Statements

In the fall of 1983, the decision was made to merge the two colleges, Southern Bible College, Houston, Texas and Evangelical Christian College, Fresno, California. This merger represented the formation of a new center of learning named "Messenger College." It is located in Joplin, Missouri and offers studies both in general and Bible subjects ideally, and is a nationally sponsored college. Property was secured directly across the street from the new Headquarters facility as a site for Messenger College.

All our resources are pooled and dedicated toward "Proclaiming Bible Truth in Pentecostal Power."

Doctrinally, the Pentecostal Church of God is a Bible based, evangelical, philosophically conservative movement, preaching and teaching God's Word in Pentecostal power with a world vision for lost mankind. We espouse and support the holiness view among our constituency and pray for the unity of purpose in fulfilling the Great Commission. We support the teaching of the Trinity Godhead; the pretribulation rapture of the Church; the new birth; the baptism of the Holy Ghost; water baptism by immersion and divine healing which are doctrinal views of the movement. We take a definite stand against all forms of immorality and indecency, unbecoming to the Christian faith. We will not frequent those places of amusement which would dishonor Christ or hinder our Christian testimony. We oppose and abstain from all forms of alcoholic beverages, hallucinative drugs and tobacco and all forms of moral perversion.

"As we observe the erosion of moral standards on every hand, we must reaffirm our desire to uphold the biblical standards against all forms of

Administrative Resource Manual

worldliness. We urge all believers to 'Love not the world, neither the things that are in the world... For all that is in the world, the lust of the flesh, and the lust of the eyes, and the pride of life, is not of the Father, but is of the world' (1 John 2:15, 16). The Scripture warns against: participation in activity which defiles the body or corrupts the mind and spirit; the inordinate love of, or preoccupation with, pleasures, positions or possessions, which lead to their misuse; any manifestation of extreme behavior, unbecoming speech or inappropriate appearances. Any fascination or association which lessens our affection for spiritual things."

For further information refer to our doctrinal statement in the General Constitution and Bylaws and the book entitled *Basic Bible Truth*.

Governmentally, the Pentecostal Church of God is "representative and congregational." Neither totally representative nor congregational it combines the two. No church, district or department is sovereign or autonomous.

The General Constitution and Bylaws state that a local church is self-governing and may adopt its own bylaws, so long as they do not conflict (disagree) with the district or General Constitution and Bylaws. Likewise the district is self-governing and may adopt its own bylaws so long as they do not conflict (disagree) with the General Constitution and Bylaws.

These things which tie us together as an organization are our mutual faith, unity of purpose and vision, harmony of doctrine, general, district and local levels of coordination and operation, form of government, fellowship and ministry.

The local congregations exercise their voice and vote in the selection of their leadership and repre-

Historical - Doctrinal - Governmental Statements

sentation to the local and district levels. The districts exercise their voice and vote in the selection of their representation to the district and General levels. The local and district, as well as General representatives, exercise a voice and vote as representatives of the entire constituency in the General Convention as the legislative body of the Church. The General Convention is the highest policy making body in the movement. The actions taken by the General Convention shall be binding upon the organization in every respect. All officials, both general and district, as well as all boards and committees, shall be bound by this action. The vote of the General Convention shall not be altered, changed or ignored by any general official, board or committee and can only be changed by a succeeding General Convention with a two-thirds (2/3) vote.

The General Convention is the legislative body. The General Board (Corporate Board of Directors) is the policy making and governing board, whose policy and actions are in accord with the General Constitution and Bylaws. The Executive Committee is a committee of the General Board empowered to act for and on behalf of the Board between regular board meetings. The corporate officers (General Superintendent and Secretary) are responsible for the administrative business of the corporation to direct, manage and supervise its function, to sign all legal documents and record the same. The Executive Committee functions as an administrative and interpretive committee of General Board policy and General Convention action. The General Superintendent has the responsibility for supervision, direction and management over all undertakings and operations of the organization. He is Corpo-

Administrative Resource Manual

rate President and is accountable to the General Board and General Convention.

The ministries of the organization are instituted by General Convention action, coordinated nationally, promoted by the districts and participated in by the local churches.

Each district, upon reaching ten or more in its overall number of established churches, may incorporate and hold property in its own name in order to propagate its work and ministry. It is recommended that all church related properties, whenever possible, be deeded to the district corporation, preferably a full deed, in order to preserve their use for the ministry of Pentecostal Church of God.

Each minister is directly accountable and amenable to his district board in all matters of faith and conduct. The district board shall exercise any disciplinary action to be taken according to provision in the district and General Constitution and Bylaws. Each minister shall be credentialed with the district and accountable to the same.

Each member of the local church is to work in harmony within the framework of the local church structure and the district. The pastor is the spiritual head of the church.

The form of government is to facilitate the philosophy and purpose of the organization and not to bring undue burden upon any member. The democratic process functions through this form of government, and we shall always give place to the instruction of God's Word and the leadership of the Holy Spirit.

Each church, as well as each district, should adopt and maintain a current set of bylaws that do not conflict with either level of operation. Each

Historical - Doctrinal - Governmental Statements

member and minister will be more cooperative with our program and work when clearly informed of the procedure and governing rules.

Administrative Resource Manual

CHAPTER 5
Organizational Structure

Organization is "the systematic arrangement of relating parts." Structure is "the manner of building, constructing or organizing; the arrangement or interrelation of all the parts as a whole; something composed of interrelating parts forming an organization." Together, organizational structure (organization and structure) is "the manner and arrangement of the interrelating parts forming the whole."

As you will recall, in the 1983 General Convention Report of the Study Committee on Structural Evaluation, we illustrated the fact of some needed changes. One of the corrections called for is in the terminology of the General Constitution and Bylaws. As an example, the Bylaws refer to the general, district and local organizations and the PYPA and Women's Ministries Departments as organizations. While this may be unimportant when proper perspective is maintained, it could lead to the misconception that these areas are independent entities rather than interrelating parts of the whole organization or denomination. I emphasize this to explain the organizational structure and its func-

Organizational Structure

tion as it now is, as opposed to how it should be ideally.

Historically, we had grown to a dozen well organized districts before we gave strength to the national administration and coordination level. Hence some re-education has been necessary.

Presently there is less struggle to understand and cooperate with the general organization than at any other time. We are maturing and becoming more effective as we communicate and coordinate all our levels and departmental ministry efforts and move together in the same direction.

At the top of every functional structure chart on the general level is the General Board, followed by the General Superintendent and a Director or President. All successive areas involved in the individual level or ministry are arranged in the proper functional order.

When building a structural chart (which is an organizational description) of any given level, department, etc., you normally begin with the responsible leader. However, if the leader reports to or is responsible to a person or group above him, then that name supersedes and should be at the top of the chart.

Of course we know that everyone is accountable to someone in a proper organization. We succeed from what we inspect rather than from what we expect. Every organization needs to review and make adjustments, redefining and clarifying (as well as making some definite changes) in its organizational structure in order to function harmoniously and more effectively.

Organization: "The systematic arrangement of parts for a defined purpose." Organization provides the structure needed by a church for mobilizing its

Administrative Resource Manual

resources to move toward the attainment of its basic spiritual purpose. Organizational structure is a means to an end rather than an end in itself. Organization provides handles whereby a church involves its members meaningfully in its life and work. Organization enables a church to group its work into manageable parts.

Some persons express a distrust of organization. Others voice the opinion that churches have too much organizational structure. These individuals, unfortunately, do not understand organization.

Organization is similar to digestion, for it works quietly and effectively in performing its unique purpose. An individual, for example, does not think about his digestive processes until he suffers a malfunction. The problem then has become one of indigestion rather than digestion.

So it is with the church organizational structure. When organization becomes oppressively apparent, the problem is usually one of disorganization rather than organization.

Following are nine principles to help our church organize for growth:

- Keep organizational structure as simple as possible.
- Group similar jobs or work together.
- Keep organizational structure as flexible as possible.
- Organizational structure should help to achieve goals.
- Organization should provide for optimum communication.

Organizational Structure

- Provide each organization and organizational leader a written statement of responsibilities.
- Organizational structure should allow decisions to be made at appropriate levels.
- Develop and provide a written organizational chart.
- Develop and provide a written job description for each person within the organizational structure.   —*Howard B. Foshee*

To illustrate, we have included:

- The General Structural Chart.
- A proposed district structural chart.
- A proposed local church structural chart.

Administrative Resource Manual

Pentecostal Church of God
National Organizational Chart

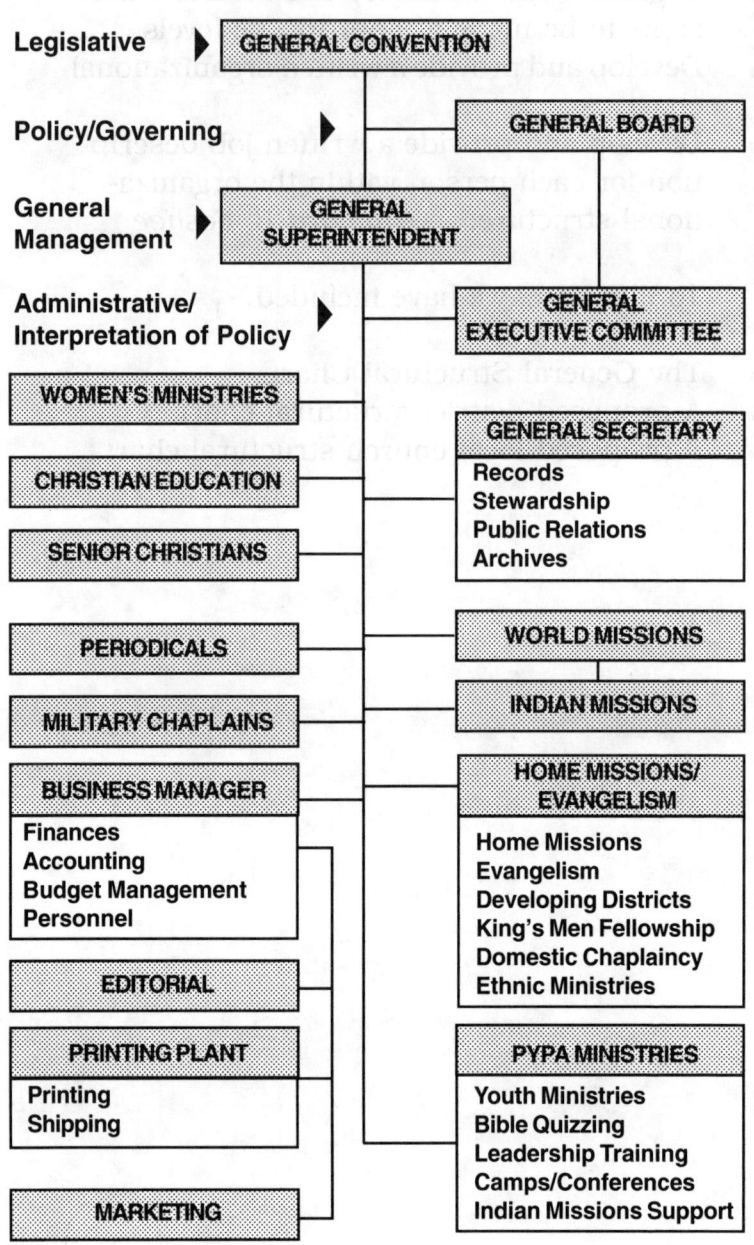

Pentecostal Church of God
District Organizational Chart

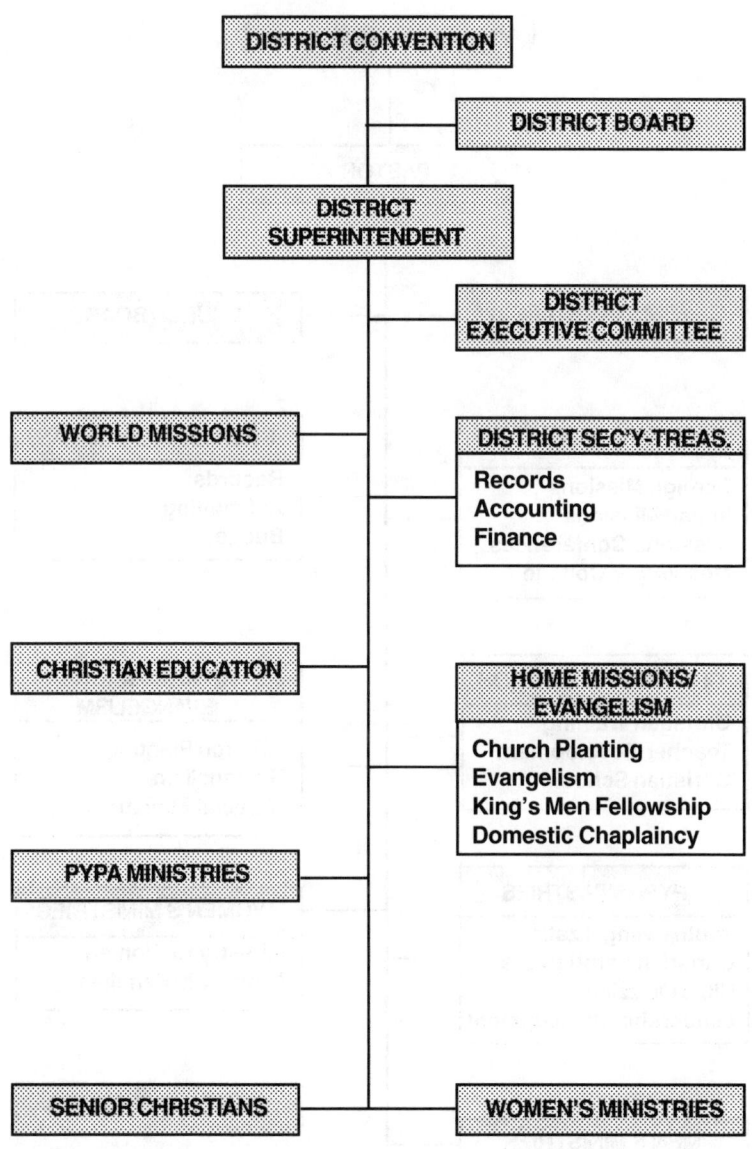

Administrative Resource Manual

Pentecostal Church of God
Local Church Organizational Chart

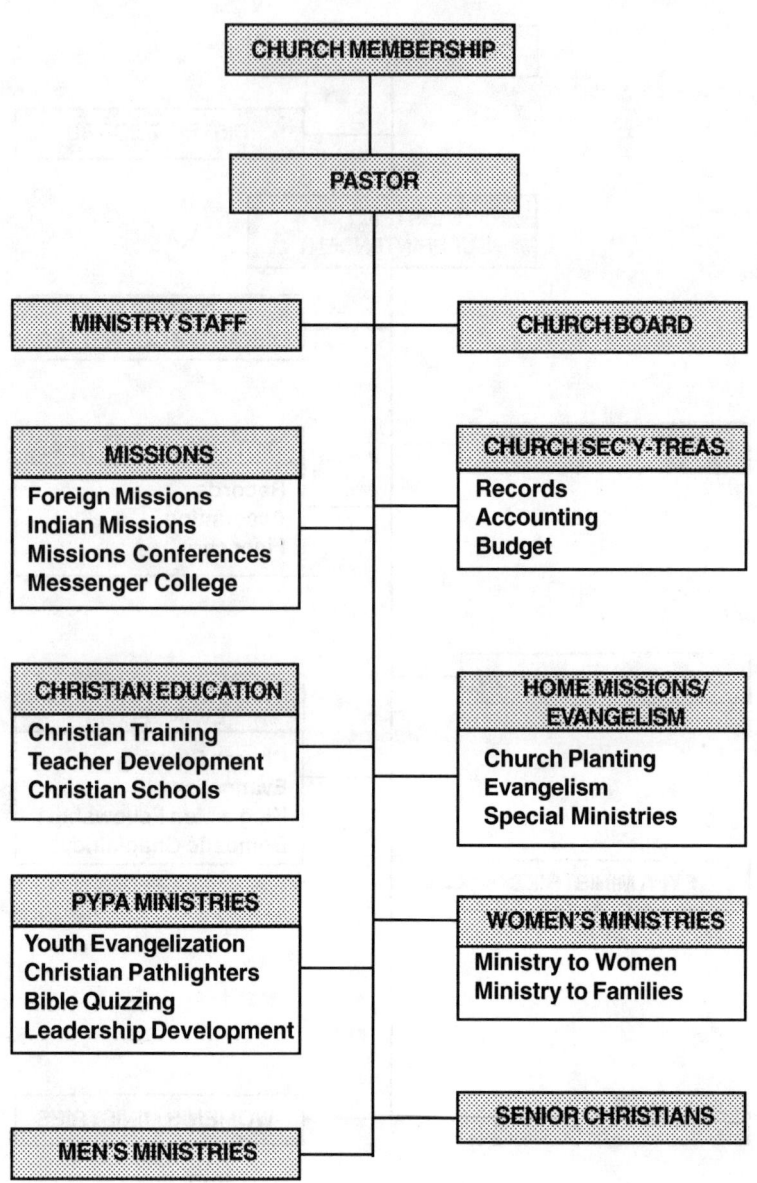

CHAPTER 6
Affiliate Memberships

The Pentecostal Church of God has a clear position of non-discrimination against any member of the Body of Christ.

And, in fact, we have found that it enhances our ministry and achievement of purpose to fellowship and cooperate with those evangelical and Pentecostal bodies which subscribe to the cardinal doctrines and basic purposes that we believe and teach.

Knowing that no man is an island, and experiencing the mutual benefits of affiliate memberships, by being a resource to one another, we have current membership in: The National Association of Evangelicals, The Evangelical Press Association, The Pentecostal World Conference, The Pentecostal/Charismatic Churches of North America, The International Pentecostal Press Association, The American Bible Society.

We have active membership and representation in leadership positions, boards and commissions of the affiliate body, receiving and being a resource for development and growth.

Administrative Resource Manual

The press affiliations provide a resource for our publications ministry by Messenger Publishing House.

The American Bible Society assists our world ministry by providing Scripture publications in various forms for spiritual life development and evangelism.

The National Association of Evangelicals (NAE) is a voluntary fellowship of evangelical denominations, churches, organizations, institutions, and individuals, demonstrating unity in the body of Christ by standing for biblical truth, speaking with a representative voice, and serving the evangelical community through united action, cooperative ministry, and strategic planning.

The association is comprised of approximately 43,000 congregations nationwide from 49 member denominations and individual congregations from an additional 27 denominations and fellowships, as well as several hundred independent churches. The membership of the association includes over 250 parachurch ministries and educational institutions. These ministries represent a broad range of theological traditions, but all subscribe to the distinctly evangelical NAE Statement of Faith. Through the cooperative ministry of these members, the National Association of Evangelicals directly and indirectly benefits over 27 million people. The association is a nationally recognized entity by the public sector with a reputation for integrity and effective service.

The cooperative ministries of the National Association of Evangelicals demonstrate the association's intentional desire to promote — *"In essentials unity, in distinctives liberty, in all things charity."*

Affiliate Memberships

IN WHAT DOES NAE BELIEVE?

The ongoing strength and vitality of NAE is explained, in part, by its seven-point statement of faith descriptive of the true evangelical. In a sense, the statement is exclusive — but only of those who do not accept the Bible as the written Word of God. Indeed, Bible-believing Christians of almost every denomination have unreservedly rallied around this unchanging statement of faith since its ratification in 1942.

1. We believe the Bible to be the inspired, the only infallible, authoritative Word of God.
2. We believe that there is one God, eternally existent in three persons: Father, Son and Holy Spirit.
3. We believe in the deity of our Lord Jesus Christ, in His virgin birth, in His sinless life, in His miracles, in His vicarious and atoning death through His shed blood, in His bodily resurrection, in His ascension to the right hand of the Father, and in His personal return in power and glory.
4. We believe that for the salvation of lost and sinful man, regeneration by the Holy Spirit is absolutely essential.
5. We believe in the present ministry of the Holy Spirit by whose indwelling the Christian is enabled to live a godly life.
6. We believe in the resurrection of both the saved and the lost; they that are saved unto the resurrection of life and they that are lost unto the resurrection of damnation.
7. We believe in the spiritual unity of believers in our Lord Jesus Christ.

GOVERNMENTAL AFFAIRS:

The Office of Public Affairs in Washington, D.C. keeps watch on legislation and works to correct any infringement of religious liberty. Evangelicals are periodically updated on these legislative developments in the publication, NAE Washington Insight. By maintaining liaison with the U.S. and foreign governments, this office has become an effective voice in behalf of evangelicals in this country and those in missionary service overseas.

PENTECOSTAL/CHARISMATIC CHURCHES OF NORTH AMERICA

The Pentecostal Church of God holds active membership in PCCNA and participates in the purpose of the fellowship. The following information is shared to better acquaint our leadership with the purpose and objectives of PCCNA.

OBJECTIVES:

It was the conviction of all who took part in the constitutional convention October 26-28, 1948, Des Moines, Iowa that there is a basic fellowship of all Pentecostal believers because of the universal belief in and experience of a personal baptism in the Holy Spirit, which is evidenced by inspirational utterance in "other tongues." That, although there has come into existence a number of organized groups of Pentecostal people, these groups have the same objectives, viz., the proclamation of a full gospel message to the ends of the world; and there should, therefore, be a basis for cooperation and fellowship. This was accomplished by creation of the Pentecostal/Charismatic Churches of North America.

Affiliate Memberships

Among the objectives of the Fellowship the following were given special mention:

1. To provide a vehicle of expression and coordination of efforts in matters common to all member bodies, including missionary and evangelistic effort throughout the world.
2. To demonstrate to the world the essential unity of spirit-baptized believers, fulfilling the prayer of the Lord Jesus "that they all may be one" (John 17:21).
3. To provide services to its constituents which will enable them to accomplish more quickly and efficiently their responsibility for the speedy evangelization of the world.
4. To encourage the principles of comity for the nurture of the Body of Christ, endeavoring to keep the unity of the Spirit until we all come to the unity of the faith.

The purpose of the fellowship is to give expression to the inherent principles of spiritual unity and fellowship of Pentecostal believers, leaving inviolate the existing forms of church government adopted by its members; and recognizing that every freedom and privilege enjoyed by any church or group of churches shall remain their undisturbed possession.

PROGRESS:

The association of member church groups in the Pentecostal/Charismatic Churches of North America has resulted in definite benefit to all. Local chapters have been formed in a number of communities where churches of the member groups are located, and fellowship rallies are held with mutual profit. On the national level, representatives of the member bodies are assembled for studies and exchange of views in the fields of home missions, foreign missions and youth. The principles of comity are being observed with due consideration of rights of local churches in any given community.

DOCTRINES:

There is evidence of remarkable unity in doctrine in all member bodies but it was thought well to draw up a statement of truth to which all should subscribe, as follows:

1. We believe the Bible to be the inspired, the only infallible authoritative Word of God.
2. We believe that there is one God, eternally existent in three persons: Father, Son and Holy Ghost.
3. We believe in the Deity of our Lord Jesus Christ, in His virgin birth, in His sinless life, in His miracles, in His vicarious and atoning sacrifice through His shed blood, in His bodily resurrection, in His ascension to the right hand of the Father, and in His personal return in power and glory.
4. We believe that for the salvation of lost and sinful men regeneration by the Holy Spirit is absolutely essential.
5. We believe that the full gospel includes holiness of heart and life, healing for the body and the baptism in the Holy Spirit with the initial evidence of speaking in other tongues as the Spirit gives utterance.
6. We believe in the present ministry of the Holy

Affiliate Memberships

Spirit by whose indwelling the Christian is enabled to live a godly life.
7. We believe in the resurrection of both the saved and the lost; they that are saved unto the resurrection of life and they that are lost unto the resurrection of damnation.
8. We believe in the spiritual unity of believers in our Lord Jesus Christ.

MEMBERSHIP:

Membership is available to those Pentecostal institutions, churches and groups of churches which shall subscribe to the Statement of Faith of the Association, and which agree to be governed by the principles, purposes and objectives of the fellowship as set forth in its constitution and bylaws.

Primarily, membership has been obtained by organized church groups of Pentecostal faith, including most recognized Pentecostal organizations and many Charismatic/independant churches.

PENTECOSTAL WORLD CONFERENCE

ORIGIN

At the turn of the century there came into existence a spiritual renaissance which took on the appellation of a Pentecostal Movement. From a small beginning in an obscure Bible School in the state of Kansas, the movement spread over the United States of America, leaped the oceans, and became established in almost every country of the world.

The movement was characterized by a belief in the restoration of New Testament *pneumatika* (spirituals) to the church, made possible through personal baptism in the Holy Spirit. The evidence of having received the Holy Spirit in Pentecostal fullness was declared to be the speaking in other tongues as the Holy Spirit gave utterance (Acts 2:4).

With one or two exceptions, the movement developed outside organized Protestantism, but attracted into its ranks spiritually hungry believers of all faiths, including Methodist, Presbyterian, Baptist, Christian and Missionary Alliance, Holiness Associations, Episcopalian and even Catholic. The denominational churches for the most part rejected the movement, which caused its advocates to engage in intensive campaigns of evangelism outside the established churches, in brush arbors in rural areas, in tents, mission halls and auditoriums. Many churches of Pentecostal faith came into being as a result. Missionaries, backed by local congregations, crossed the seas to evangelize as early as 1906. The result was that the Pentecostal Movement took hold in China, India, South Africa, Brazil, Chile and other countries, and by the year 1909, had taken root in England, Sweden, Norway and Germany. During the first ten years, the movement had become world-wide.

In the beginning, there was an antipathy to any form of organization, but gradually, groups of Pentecostal believers became associated in fellowships by various names, so that by the year 1914, several organized groups began to emerge. These groups had much in common so far as doctrinal belief is concerned, but they developed independently of each other. As a consequence they often found themselves in conflict with the churches of other groups, especially in local areas, which was to be deplored.

The first step taken, looking forward to unity of spirit and cooperative fellowship of all Pentecostal bodies, was in the year 1946, when a call was is-

Affiliate Memberships

sued for a World Conference of Pentecostal believers to be held in Zurich, Switzerland, in the month of May, 1947. At that conference, Pentecostal representatives of many groups in 22 countries were assembled.

It was an exploratory meeting and served as a forerunner for the following subsequent World Conferences: 1949, Paris; 1952, London; 1955, Stockholm; 1958, Toronto; 1961, Jerusalem; 1964 Helsinki; 1967, Rio de Janeiro; 1970, Dallas; 1973, Seoul; 1976, London; 1979, Vancouver; 1982, Kenya; 1985, Zurich; 1988, Singapore; 1991, Norway ; 1995, Jerusalem; 1998, Seoul.

The success of the first world conference held in Switzerland served as the inspiration for an effort to bring together the organized bodies of Pentecostal believers in the United States of America. Following two preliminary meetings, with participation by representatives of ten or more organized Pentecostal communions, the constitutional convention of the Pentecostal Fellowship of North America was convened in Des Moines, Iowa, October 26-28, 1948. The PFNA was absorbed in the Pentecostal/Charismatic Churches of North America in an historic meeting in Memphis between the black Pentecostal bodies and the predominantly white PFNA in 1994.

Administrative Resource Manual

- SECTION TWO -
PROGRAM ADMINISTRATION

A program can be seen as the concrete results of effective planning. It all begins with vision from which we derive our mission. Only when the vision and mission are clearly understood are we in a position to formulate plans, beginning with the long range plan and breaking this into incremental plans. Your plan will shape your program.

Special emphasis and detail is given here on "how to" in the areas of planning and conducting a district convention, as always, pursuing excellence in God's work. This program may serve as a model for local and other programs.

The administration of the district office, planning and conducting meetings and information on performing ceremonies are also a part of this section.

These chapters make up Section Two:

Chapter 7 -   Program of Ministry
Chapter 8 -   District Office Administration
Chapter 9 -   Legal/Technical Information
Chapter 10 - Planning and Conducting
              a District Convention
Chapter 11 - Mr. Chairman -
              Chairing the Business Session
Chapter 12 - Officiating at Ceremonies

CHAPTER 7
Program of Ministry

A motivational speaker in Detroit had an unusual closing to his speech. He began by telling of his experience with the Rubik's cube. It seemed the young son had mastered the cube but the father had experienced only frustration in trying to work the device. The son revealed to his father that he had purchased the instruction booklet which was his source for success. He said, "Dad, there are 49,000 ways to do it wrong. But if you want to succeed, you must go to the book."

Life is that way. If you don't know where you are going, any road will get you there. But if you want life and work to come together, you must go to the Book, the Bible.

In the introduction, we listed the four-fold priority of the church as being purpose, people, program and property. The program is the method by which we administer the work.

The program is the organized method by which you reach the purpose. The church's most-used term is "ministries." The program is explained and it

Administrative Resource Manual

functions through various ministries coordinated into related sections, divisions or departments.

To illustrate, the district is made up of various ministries and programs. The leader plans the schedule of events to highlight and promote the various aspects of the program.

The district meetings are designed for fellowship, communication and instruction as well as to inspire and motivate. The goal is to see every member become a participant and supporter of the ministry program.

The ministries that we wish to acquaint our people with and to see them support are the general church ministries, initiated by the general organization through the years, such as: Missions - Foreign, Indian and Home; Hispanic Missions and special ministries; Christian Education — the National Sunday School Program and Christian Day School ministry, Bible college and higher Christian Education; Church Ministries — in the areas of youth (Pentecostal Young People's Association), ladies (Women's Ministries), men (King's Men Fellowship), seniors (Senior Christian Fellowship), the military chaplaincy and publications ministry.

HISTORY OF MINISTRIES
MISSIONS MINISTRIES:

World Missions had its beginning in 1932 though our records show that missionary offerings were sent overseas in the early 1920s. We have carried the gospel message to over 65 countries. Presently, the Pentecostal Church of God has established 3,109 churches and 57 Bible schools in more than 47 countries. The sun never sets on this ongoing full gospel ministry.

Program of Ministry

Indian Missions was established in 1949 and is sponsored by the youth of our movement. Presently, 180 buildings have been built on reservations. More than 90 preaching sites are established with 110 full time missionaries ministering to more than 78 tribes of the North American Indians,

Hispanic Missions: For more than 20 years our border missions efforts have produced approximately 20 works among the Spanish speaking people of America, which is seed for an abundant harvest in the future. We are now beginning to plant new works further inland into the United States.

Home Missions/Evangelism: In 1981, the establishment of the National Home Missions/Evangelism program became a reality. Heretofore, our Home Missions/Evangelism efforts have been on a district level. By this national effort, it is our aim to broaden and strengthen our base for world evangelism, and to assist our districts in their efforts of Home Missions.

CHRISTIAN EDUCATION MINISTRIES:

In 1954, the department of Christian Education was established. However, in the area of curriculum, we began producing our Sunday school material in 1939. The Christian Education department is expressed in three area divisions.

National Sunday School Program: Coordinating on the national, district and local church levels, this program provides the necessary administration, leadership, teacher development and curriculum for more than 1600 Sunday schools. The National Board of Christian Education exists to coordinate this important arm of ministry.

Christian Schools: A developing area of Christian Education using church related facilities, which

Administrative Resource Manual

is bringing Biblical principles back into education as was originally included in public education.

Bible Colleges: To reseed and insure the perpetuation of our ministry, we have merged our two Bible colleges, Evangelical Christian College in Fresno, California and Southern Bible College in Houston, Texas into the newly formed Messenger College located in Joplin, Missouri.

CHURCH MINISTRIES:

Pentecostal Young People's Association was organized in 1928, and has functioned under the banner of "Victory Thru Christ Around the World" to this time. It's ministry includes an emphasis on Indian Missions, Bible Quizzing, Christian Pathlighters, Youth Evangelism in Action and Leadership Development. It is a viable ministry of the church.

Women's Ministries was established in 1956 with a purpose to minister to the total woman through evangelization and spiritual enrichment. It is an auxiliary ministry sharing a missionary zeal throughout the church and the world. The motto is, "Labourers Together with God."

King's Men Fellowship: This fellowship began as a national program in 1975 and seeks to win men for Christ, to train them and to utilize this vast reservoir of great strength for our Lord and the Church.

Senior Christian Fellowship was organized in 1981 to provide an opportunity for fellowship, further involvement and interaction on peer level and as a continuing resource for world evangelism for all of those over 60 years of age.

Program of Ministry

MESSENGER PUBLICATIONS:

The Messenger Publishing House has produced Bible oriented literature since the inception of the movement. Our official publication, *The Pentecostal Messenger, Spirit* magazine, gospel tracts, books, Sunday school educational materials, by-laws, Minister's Study Series and many miscellaneous pieces produced annually continue to play a vital role in our effort of gospel distribution and publishing the good news to all lands. Messenger Publishing House is an affiliate member of the Evangelical Press Association and the International Pentecostal Press Association.

MILITARY CHAPLAINCY:

Being a member of the Commission on Chaplains of the National Association of Evangelicals, this commission becomes our official endorsing agency. Our chaplaincy program operates under the Pentecostal Church of God Commissions on Military Chaplains.

In addition to the program of various ministries, we plan special leadership enrichment and development meetings of interest through seminars and conferences.

Administrative Resource Manual

PROGRAM DESIGN

How is your program design? Do you feel that the many activities and much time spent could be better programmed for effectiveness? If so evaluation is in order. In our administrative work, there must be this continuing process of evaluation in order to be more effective and better stewards of God's program.

Refer to the structural chart for a perspective of the program at work. Fine tuning will be needed in a continuing effort to improve the program. Your program should be evaluated and adjusted as needed for best results.

There is a better way to do most everything if we can find it. Therefore, as administrators, we are in a continuing school of learning and pursuit for excellence. If it is true that anything worth doing is worth doing well, then this should surely apply to the Lord's work.

There are similarities in administration on three levels—church, district and general—as the ministries are quite similar. Some levels are broader and more technical. Life is a challenge and so is this exciting work of administration. Let us seek to excel in all we do for His Kingdom.

CHAPTER 8
District Office Administration

The district office is as the hub to a wheel on the district level. It is the center of service and coordination of the district activity. As soon as a district can organize a central district office, the better that district can function. All records, departmental function and business administration require the need of a central district office.

The district superintendent is the chief executive administrative officer of the district and district office. He must schedule regular business hours in the office for district business. Many officers find this difficult to do, but it is absolutely necessary as no office operates by itself. A major duty of the superintendent is that of office manager. His overall effectiveness will be reflected by his business and administrative expertise.

The district superintendent must be acquainted with the various functions of the district office. Although work is delegated, he must supervise. He directs, manages and supervises all the district functions.

Administrative Resource Manual

As the corporate president, the superintendent is chairman of the district board. The district board is the corporate board of directors. The board relies upon the superintendent for leadership so they, together, may govern the affairs of the district according to purpose and objectives set forth in the Constitution and Bylaws.

As the chairman of the board, the superintendent is a resource person on all matters of structure, policy, procedure, history and program. And, as the Scripture admonishes, we are to be ready always to give an answer to every man.

One learns quickly in office that it is not absolutely necessary to know everything on every subject. Yet, a leader needs to be able to locate and know his resources, whether people or materials, and consult them when in need. There is a resource for all your needs which you may draw upon for assistance.

Communication is a vital element to the harmony and success of the district program. It is well to be in touch with the district board members and pastors in whatever ways which serve best. One effective way is to be present in sectional and local church meetings. Another way is through a newsletter or similar form. An informed constituency is a supportive constituency. Supplies are available as aids for communicating the program and ministries.

Coordination of effort is another vital task for successful implementation of the various phases of the district program. The individual ministry or function cannot be allowed to operate independently of the general purpose of the whole. But all parts are to be centrally coordinated and move forward harmoniously in the direction of the general pur-

District Office Administration

pose of the district and general organization. We must pull together lest we find ourselves pulling apart and our cause be frustrated.

The district superintendent is the coordinator of the district program and ministry.

CHAPTER 9
Legal/Technical Information

We live in an unprecedented time when we must be adept in business procedures in the district office as we serve and service each church and minister in the district.

Legal matters and documents, as well as orderly files and records, are demanded more today than at any other time. The district secretary-treasurer performs a vital service for the district in this area. He also plays a supportive role to the superintendent in communication and by organizing and maintaining a current record of legal and other needed information.

There should be copies of the original articles of incorporation with the state; a complete file of minutes of all district conventions and board meetings; a current file of ministers and churches in an orderly system for quick reference. Legal papers on properties properly drawn and filed are an important part of corporate business.

Legal/Technical Information

A history of the district with its beginning and growth and those serving in office should be a matter of file by the secretary.

It is extremely important that the district superintendent and secretary-treasurer develop a good working relationship and maintain a constant interchange of news and information within the district. A regular (monthly) meeting to review budgetary information and current status will be helpful in an ongoing effort of administration.

Since the district superintendent is ultimately responsible for all district office function, the final decision in all matters must rest with his office. Any matter not governed by clear district policy and procedure should be brought to the superintendent for his decision.

Personality or other differences between corporate officers must be set aside in the best interest of the work. We must not traffic in trivia while priority district work goes wanting. There can and should be a mutual respect between these officers.

A successful program must have coordination of efforts, communication of goals and participation by all members. Though you may persevere, with burden and vision, you as a leader, achieve success only as you inspire cooperation of your constituency in the program. These three key words are used over and over again, "Inspire - Instruct - Involve." This then is our task in administration on almost all levels. May our performance be such as to inspire vision and accomplish mission, utilizing all available resources to achieve our purpose.

How long has it been since you reviewed your file of legal documents and technical information? You will need to update these.

Administrative Resource Manual

- Articles of Incorporation
- Registration with State and Federal Governments
- Tax Exemption Requirements
- Deeds to Properties - appropriately filed
- Forms and Certificates needed
- Ministers Files
- Churches and Other Properties
- Current Financial Statement and Net Worth
- Membership Roll and Related Data
- Office Administration and Procedural Matters clearly written and filed

Annual Schedules

Each district office must have a legal attorney for consultation should the need arise. Limited knowledge in this area can be disastrous when erroneous decisions are made as a result of not securing such necessary legal counsel.

We often find ourselves thrust into real estate dealings, the securing of loans and advising and counseling people in such related matters, and/or developing financial statements, budgets and other fiscal matters. The responsibility of caring for the churches and ministries demands established principal procedures, appropriate documents and technical data to aid in management. Our business must be performed in a business-like manner to insure satisfying results.

Concerning property deeds, experience teaches us that whenever possible we should have a full deed with the district corporation, instead of a joint deed. There can be conflicting verbiage in the joint deed that may not be in the movement's best interest in matters going to litigation.

Legal/Technical Information

If for some reason a deed or one-half joint deed is returned to the church, include a legally binding reversionary clause to secure the property for the perpetuation of our ministry. Unfortunately there are those who feel no wrong in confiscating property dedicated to this ministry.

One area of concern which has caused confusion is that some district bylaws have carried the words autonomous or sovereign in reference to the local church. Neither our General Constitution and Bylaws nor General Board Policy support this. The church is self-governing and is not to be in conflict with the district or general organization. There is no rule above anything sovereign and clearly we are all accountable, whether it be an individual, church, district or general organization.

Also, when the district is endorsing a loan for a local church it is wise to insure that the local property and assets provide security for the loan (whenever possible) so as not to obligate all corporate assets.

CHAPTER 10
Planning and Conducting a District Convention

Among the many duties of the district superintendent is that of planning, coordinating and conducting the district convention. This is the most important district meeting in terms of effort in planning and implementing. It is highly technical, yet inspiring and is most meaningful of all meetings. Most superintendents leave these meetings exhausted because of intense concentration and concern. They find themselves filling the role of an answer man and a resource person to all committees and functions, often performing numerous menial tasks.

The district convention is a meeting where we hear reports of progress and performance; where we process necessary district business, such as approving needed bylaw amendments and conducting elections of officers. It is a time to gauge our performance of ministry and to reevaluate our dedication to God.

Planning and Conducting a District Convention
PLANNING AND PROMOTING THE MEETING

Planning and organization should be done early enough to properly promote and publicize the meeting for maximum attendance and participation. Serving as the meeting planner, the superintendent needs to select or have selected the city and location of the meeting well in advance of the appointed date. If the convention is to be in a local church then the local presbyter and pastors can serve along with the superintendent in planning and preparing necessary functions and services for the meeting. It is wise to compile a check list of items that need attention such as:

- Adequate Auditorium Facility
- Proper Heating/Air Conditioning for Comfort
- Sufficient Number of Committee Rooms
- Area Meal Function Locations
- Parking Areas
- Materials Showing Area Services
- Nursery Facilities
- Musical Instruments
- Public Announcement System and Taping Equipment
- Arrange and Decorate Platform
- Special Plans for Ordination and Memorial Services
- Offering Buckets and Teller Room
- Ballots for Elections
- Lodging for Officers and Guests
- Registration Materials and Area
- Advance Publicity
- Message Center During Meetings
- Telephone Service
- Exhibit Space

Administrative Resource Manual

- Banners and Signs Space
- Needed Office Equipment
- Safety Features of Building
- Ample Comfort Stations
- Printed Materials
- Song Books

This check list will need additional items included. Things forgotten will cause last minute problems. You need to anticipate and prepare for everything possible in advance to insure a successful meeting.

To help the superintendent in a district convention, it is wise to eliminate all district board meetings during a convention whenever possible.

The budget should be planned well in advance with the Finance Committee and offering recording sheets having been printed to help the tellers quickly count and prepare a report (sample under miscellaneous). It is wise to anticipate and plan to receive offerings during the progress of the meetings and sessions of the convention so that the greater part of the budget will have been raised before the last services. Those to receive the offerings need to be apprised early.

SELECTING THE COMMITTEES

It is customary for the district superintendent to appoint committees to assist him in the convention. This should be done in draft form four months prior to the convention. The district bylaws usually provide for a minimum list of committees needed. However, the superintendent may name additional committees as needed. The superintendent, at his discretion, may share his list of appointed committees with his district board for their input.

Planning and Conducting a District Convention

The necessary committees to serve the convention are:

- Registration Committee
- Rules of Order Committee
- Entertainment Committee
- Program Committee
- Publicity Committee
- Resolutions Committee
- Memorial Committee
- Finance Committee
- Auditing Committee
- Others

It is wise for the district superintendent to plan an orientation session with the chairmen of all committees prior to the meeting.

CONVENTION COMMITTEES AND THEIR FUNCTIONS

There should be a chairman and an alternate chairman. It is not necessary to use the term chairperson. There should be an appropriate number on each committee that usually attend the convention.

REGISTRATION COMMITTEE:

The chairman normally is the district secretary/treasurer because his office contains the information needed to qualify delegates for the convention. He will need reliable assistance yet he supplies the information needed to qualify delegates. He leads the committee in early orientation on criteria and instructions for registration. He provides the supplies and equipment needed. He reports the results of registration to the body.

The function of this committee is to see that all potential delegates are properly registered according to established qualifications. There must be good order and clear instructions given to each committee member assisting with registration otherwise confusion can linger throughout the convention beginning at the registration table. Any question not clearly answered in registration instructions or decision needed other than that of the committee chairman is decided by the credentials committee.

RULES OF ORDER COMMITTEE:

The chairman is a person knowledgeable of the bylaws, rules of order and procedure. He shall call his committee to order before any business of the convention to review the bylaw provisions and procedural requirements for the convention. He presents the recommended rules to the convention for consideration.

The function of this committee is to review all sources of rules, bylaws, etc. related to the processing of church business; to organize and delegate the typing of appropriate copies of the recommended rules to govern the business sessions. The rules should be sufficient but not cumbersome and should not refer to areas unrelated to our style of convention. The rules can be amended by the convention if needed. The rules of order should contain the bylaw provisions covering percentages of vote to pass measures or elect officers.

The constituency should thoroughly understand procedure, for we suffer more ill from a misunder-

Planning and Conducting a District Convention

standing or lack of understanding than from direct opposition.

The General Constitution and Bylaws carry a good recommended rules of order as a reference. (Listed under the section on Procedure are recommended rules of order for district conventions.)

ENTERTAINMENT COMMITTEE:

If the convention is being conducted in one of our churches, then normally the pastor will serve as the chairman of the committee. The reason for this is that he is well acquainted with the area and can provide the convention with its needed services. However, another person could be used if a given situation demands it.

The area pastors and presbyter are members of this committee which can serve in a meaningful role with the chairman.

Functions of the committee are to coordinate a service to the convention by seeking to insure the comfort of the members with regard to facilities; to see that convenient areas and personal and community services and materials to assist the delegates are supplied. Housing is a vital role of the committee. Along with these there must be adequate planning for safety and emergency provisions should the need arise. The committee also assists with the parking.

The committee will need to meet and coordinate its work prior to the convention. It is well to entertain in such a way that the convention would be pleased to return for a future meeting.

PROGRAM COMMITTEE:

The chairman of this committee should be a person with knowledge of leading services and of delegating those to lead the various services of the convention. Upon the committee's appointments, he is to notify the various people who are to be in charge. After the committee meets, a list of the names of those to be in charge should be given to the district superintendent. The chairman is to monitor and supervise the appointments and remind program leaders of their time slots.

The function of this committee is to review the services to be held during the convention and to approve the recommendations of the chairman for these leadership positions. The committee will need to meet the first day of convention (or earlier) to perform these tasks. Alternates to be in charge of a service should be selected and on standby in the event they are needed.

PUBLICITY COMMITTEE:

This chairman should be a person capable of preparing news releases for delivery to various agencies to publicize the meeting.

The function of this committee is to organize news releases, thoroughly checking each item for accuracy and to have the information typed, double spaced and edited. The work of the committee is performed prior to the meeting. The various agencies to be used should be contacted in advance so the news item would appear on the Sunday preceding the meeting.

RESOLUTION COMMITTEE:

This chairman should be an individual experienced in this position for this committee has an important task to perform. The chairman is to apprise the committee of any conflict of a proposed

Planning and Conducting a District Convention

resolution to the bylaw. He is to direct the committee in processing and assembling. The chairman will present the resolution to the floor and unless the committee objects, he moves the adoption for discussion.

The function of this committee is to review all proposed resolutions. If there are duplicating or conflicting resolutions, the committee discusses the resolution with the author and approves the presentation of the resolutions to the convention. The Resolution Committee does not have the authority to dispose of any resolution in the committee without permission of the author. The following is an orderly way to write a resolution.

- The usual wording of a resolution is, "I move the adoption of the following resolution: 'Resolved, That . . .'" ; or, "I offer the following resolution: 'Resolved, That . . .'"
- It is usually inadvisable to attempt to include the reasons for a motion's adoption with the motion itself. Neither rule nor custom requires a resolution to have a preamble. However, special circumstances make it desirable to include a brief statement or statements of background or reasoning. In this case a preamble should be used. It generally should contain no more clauses than are absolutely necessary.
- If there is a preamble, each clause should be written as a separate paragraph, beginning with the word "Whereas" followed by a comma. The next word should begin with a capital letter. Regardless of how many paragraphs it has the preamble should never contain a period. Each of its paragraphs should close with a semicolon. In the next to the last paragraph the semi-

Administrative Resource Manual

colon should be followed by the word "and." The last paragraph of the preamble should close with a semicolon, followed by a connecting expression such as "therefore" or "therefore, be it" or "now, therefore, be it." When one of these phrases is included, no punctuation should follow it, and it should always be placed at the end of the preamble paragraph, never at the beginning of the resolving paragraph, thus:

- Whereas, The . . . (text of the preamble); now, therefore, be it
- Resolved, That . . . (stating action to be taken).
- The word "Resolved" is underlined or printed in italics. It is followed by a comma and the word "That" - which begins with a capital "T."
- There are times when more than one preamble clause and several resolving clauses are needed. In this case each should be a separate paragraph. An example of how this is handled is listed below:
  - Whereas, The . . (text of the first preamble clause);
  - Whereas, . . . (text of the next to the last preamble clause); and
  - Whereas, . . . (text of the last preamble clause);
  - Resolved, That . . . (stating action to be taken);
  - Resolved, That . . . (stating further action to be taken); and
  - Resolved, That . . . (stating still further action to be taken).

MEMORIAL COMMITTEE:

The chairman should be a person of dignity and experience who shall plan the service as soon after the convention begins as possible, contacting and

Planning and Conducting a District Convention

notifying all who participate as to schedule and placement.

The function of this committee is to assist the chairman to organize this very special service that is meaningful to all. A dignified yet warm atmosphere is desired. The reading of names of the deceased should be performed by the district secretary/treasurer.

Appropriate music, Scripture reading and comments are in order. A commemorative token honoring those departed, such as a rose placed in a bouquet by a representative or relative, has a spiritual meaning.

A timely message with prayer is always in order. Time is important. Not too long, not too short. Plan and try to stay with the plan.

FINANCE COMMITTEE:

This chairman is chosen from among those of some business acumen and ability. Many times the district presbyter is selected because of his knowledge of the district and its needs.

The chairman should introduce and explain the budget and the plan to meet the budget and should report occasionally on progress. He will see that the assistance of personnel and materials are supplied.

Function of the committee is to establish the convention budget with input from the superintendent; to organize the method of raising the funds and appointing the people needed to receive the offerings for budget.

Frequently conventions are adopting an organized budget system with the churches participating in the budget and appropriate honorariums

Administrative Resource Manual

given in lieu of love offerings to all individuals reporting or ministering in the meeting.

This can be good in that more of the constituency are participating in the budget of your meeting. However, the district superintendent should be especially honored in some way; perhaps a love offering after his report in lieu of an honorarium (as long as it is equal to or more than the honorarium), inasmuch as the full burden of the district function is on his shoulders. No other officer in the district is his equal.

AUDITING COMMITTEE:

This chairman should be knowledgeable of accounting and able, with his committee, to perform the auditing task. He works with the district secretary/treasurer to set an appropriate time before convention and notifies his committee of the date, time and place to perform the audit. He organizes the process and reports his committee's findings prior to the giving of financial reports in the convention.

The function of this committee is to check posting of the ledger with the receipts, the balancing and reconciliation of bank statements with the ledger and the disbursements and bank balances to determine if all funds are accounted for. Note should be made as to order of records, whether good or in need of improvement.

A convention announcement along with the program and a list of committees should be mailed to each minister in the district 30 days prior to the convention.

FUNCTION OF PARLIAMENTARIAN

Planning and Conducting a District Convention

The recommended rules of order for conventions call for the appointment of a parliamentary committee of three members by the superintendent.

The purpose of the committee is to assist the body and convention chairman in parliamentary procedure when called upon.

If the parliamentarians are member delegates they have delegate privileges in debate and business as other delegates.

If the rules of order authorize the committee to decide any issue of procedure that may come before the group, then a majority rule of the committee makes the final decision.

Should there be an appeal from the decision of the chair, the committee will either concur or oppose the decision, thus eliminating the necessity of appealing to the entire body.

The parliamentarians are not to engage in publicly debating procedural matters before the group at will. They are a resource, an advisory committee to function when called upon. The chairman is in charge and makes decisions and/or states decisions to the delegation.

This committee should be selected from knowledgeable men. They should be supplied with the necessary resource materials and always seated on the platform.

It is wise for the chairman to meet with the committee for orientation prior to the meeting.

One of the members is to be named chairman of the committee who shall lead the committee in its decision process.

It is wise for the convention chairman to consult with the committee on procedure when in doubt.

Administrative Resource Manual
DISTRICT CONVENTION
ORDER OF CONVENTION BUSINESS

First: Begin with a devotional using appropriate Scripture reading.

Second: Call the meeting to order—"The business meeting of the 1984 Georgia District Convention of the Pentecostal Church of God will now come to order. All actions taken by this convention are binding upon its constituency in every way." (Gavel strikes the podium.) Apprise the convention of the order of business to be conducted.

Third: Report of the Registration Committee

If registration remains open, this first report is a preliminary report. Any correction to the report? If not, the report stands approved as read.

Fourth: Report of the Rules of Order Committee

Seat the convention. Be sure those who are to assist you, according to the Rules of Order, are in place. Be sure the people understand procedures.

Fifth: Report of the District Superintendent

The Finance Committee Chairman works with the Convention Chairman as to the time for offerings to be received.

Sixth: Report of the District Secretary

This is his personal activity and membership report, if given separately. Sometimes the officer combines his report.

Seventh: Report of the Auditing Committee

If possible, the committee may give one report for the district office and all departmental records in the interest time.

Eighth: Report of the Treasurer (Financial Report)

Ninth: Report of the District Presbyter

Tenth: Other Officers Reports:

Planning and Conducting a District Convention

Sectional Presbyters
Women's Ministries (unless reported in an earlier service)
Christian Education
Home Missions
King's Men Fellowship
Others

Eleventh: Unfinished Business

Twelfth: Report of Committees
Entertainment
Program
Publicity
Memorial

Thirteenth: Report of Resolutions Committee

Remind the group of the provisions of the Rules of Order. Set all those to assist the chairman in motions: Recording Secretary, Time Keeper and Parliamentarians.

Fourteenth: Election of Officers

Fifteenth: New business (other than resolutions or amendments to bylaws)

Sixteenth: Ratifications by the Convention

Seventeenth: Adjournment

WRITING CONVENTION REPORTS:

It is very important to present an interesting report. (This is not the place to preach or to wax lengthy.) Because some either have not given well-organized reports or have diverted from their written copy, using valuable time of the convention, many reports are filed with the secretary or eliminated altogether. This should not be since one important purpose of a convention is to receive progress reports from all ministries and functions.

Administrative Resource Manual

Experience demonstrates that many leaders have not been adequately instructed on how to give a report. Perhaps this simple outline will help. The content of officers' reports will vary as their duties are not the same in every detail.

1. Title of the report
2. Opening introductory
3. Greetings
4. Activities
5. Special observations
6. Closing

Please read your report. Do not digress. If you do, do so only once briefly. Type two copies of your report, one for the district secretary/treasurer and one for your file. The title should read: "Report of the District Superintendent" (or other officer). Include the date. The introduction should not be lengthy; it is not necessary to name every person who is serving in an office or position. Instead, it should read something like this:

> "Giving honor to our Lord Jesus Christ, the Head of the Church; to the Convention Chairman; to our General Executives; to Members of the District Board, Ministers, Delegates and Guests of the 1999 District Convention now in session."

Greetings should be a brief statement or short Scripture portion. Say something like, "Greetings to one and all with prayer for God's special blessings on this gathering."

One source of opposition to presbyters' reports is that they frequently overlap with the district su-

Planning and Conducting a District Convention

perintendents' reports. That each report include every church in the section or district is not a requirement.

The report is an officer's activity report serving the respective positions. The district superintendent's report should include a general overview of the district. The presbyter's report can be a little more specific, highlighting special growth, development, etc.

Administrative Resource Manual

CHAPTER 11
Mr. Chairman — Chairing the Business Session

As the presiding officer, the chairman is the leader and representative of the district organization. Respect for him, therefore, is respect for the organization and its members who elected him. The presiding officer is correctly addressed as Mr. President or Madam President — Mr. Chairman or Madam Chairman, but he refers to himself as "The Chair". "Brother Chairman" or "Sister Chairman" should not be used.

Resolution was passed by the National Association of Parliamentarians to discourage the use of the term "Chairperson".

F. H. Kerfoot, in his book *Parliamentary Law* (pages 18-20) states,

> To be a good presiding officer, one should have quick perception and, with this, a good judicial mind, so that he may be able to see quickly all points involved and decide fairly upon all questions. He should be entirely

impartial in all his rulings, trying to give to everyone his rights. He should be thoroughly familiar with the law by which the assembly is governed. He should be a man of even temper, and one who will be at all times gentlemanly in his bearings toward everyone, and thus avoid all friction in his management of the body. He should have tact to turn aside quickly and easily the various occasions for friction that inevitably arise among members. And above all, he should be a man of promptness and firmness in all decisions.

The district superintendent is to serve as the chairman unless the General Superintendent or an alternate has been invited by the district superintendent or the district board to serve the convention as chairman of the business session. As the movement grows it will necessitate more involvement by the district superintendents to chair their respective conventions because of the demand of administrative duties on the General Superintendent at the General Office. In addition, it is a meaningful leadership developing exercise to have district leaders to perform these duties.

At this point, it must be emphasized that as a leader, you can chair the meeting successfully if you set in motion clear procedure and order and stay on course. Should you make a mistake, an apology is in order. It seems to please the people to know it is possible for the chairman to make a mistake. When he does not attempt to cover it up the group will cooperate with him. Strive to be correct and impartial without seeming to be too technical or a know-it-all. It is often difficult for a district superintendent to refrain from comment on

Administrative Resource Manual

the issues. If you feel you must do so, turn the chair to someone else, then proceed. There is nothing like practice to give you confidence.

CHAPTER 12
Officiating at Ceremonies

This chapter deals with those situations in which the leader may find himself involved because of his position. Ceremonies are very important and like so many other functions we must find balance in order to perform the task well. The ceremony can be programmed to either extreme which will hinder a successful event.

There is an abundance of minister's manuals with information and ideas on conducting ceremonies and we can use all the help available.

CONDUCTING THE ORDINATION CEREMONY

Never ordain a person who has not been sufficiently cleared for ordination by both general and district bylaws and the General Board policy with approval of the respective credential committees. If an unqualified person is ordained, it will be extremely difficult to correct the situation. Procedure must take its due course regardless of the frenzied hurry some people often get into. If you allow yourself to be pressured into making decisions and/or

Administrative Resource Manual

doing things not according to established steps of procedure, at some point you will meet with disaster; then, you will receive the blame.

Allow the Lord to lead you concerning the message and ceremony of ordination. Although we have included a sample ceremony, you may prefer to develop your own.

Notify those to be ordained of the time and particulars of the service.

Have your district board on the platform. Seat candidates and companions on front center row at the beginning of the service.

Usually the ceremony of ordination follows the sermon. However, it is well to introduce candidates to the congregation before the sermon.

Notify all those participating in the ceremony in advance: Who is to pray over those being ordained? Who is to present the certificates? Music? Apprise candidates of Scripture references, etc.

Try to create an atmosphere of dedication and commitment. Have the district board and visiting executives join you at the altar for ordination.

If you are to minister and conduct the ordination ceremony, you may find this sample ceremony helpful. It begins with an outline, follows through to the message and continues on through the concluding ceremony.

In time you will want to organize your own ceremony as the Lord leads you.

"THE ORDINATION SERVICE"
OPENING STATEMENT:
PRAYER:
MESSAGE:
CEREMONY:
FELLOWSHIP:

Officiating at Ceremonies

OPENING STATEMENT:

All Christians are equal but ministers are set apart for special full time service and leadership.

The minister is a servant and a steward, ordained (appointed and set apart) to this gospel ministry. We serve Christ as we minister Him to others. This ministry is to the establishment, edification and leadership of the church.

Ordination symbolizes God's call to the ministry, the candidate's commitment of himself to the ministry in the will of God, and the church's approval of the candidate for the ministry.

Ordination does not bestow any honor or authority on one above another. Authority and power for ministry are conferred directly by Christ, and not by those performing the ordination ceremony. Evangelicals stress an immediate spiritual connection with Christ. It is a vertical concept as opposed to a horizontal one. The Christ who is the Head of the Church is the maker of ministers. Ordination may be briefly called a public acknowledgement and confirmation of the candidate's call to this office.

As an example, the Old Testament priests were consecrated to their office by means of the anointing oil applied to their person and garments, by the laying on of hands and by prayer. Jesus called and ordained the Twelve and then the seventy. The Apostle Peter presided over the ordination of Methias to take the place of Judas. In Acts, the seven were ordained as deacons. Paul and Barnabas were ordained in Acts 13 and then they ordained pastors and elders in the churches. Paul's ordination of Timothy is outstanding of all as an example.

All these except Methias, of which the Scripture is silent, had a most successful ministry.

Ordination is not a sacrament or ordinance of the church. Our ministry priority is proclamational above sacramental, as the pulpit is always elevated above the communion table.

Briefly then, ordination is not essentially a conferral, a bestowal or an impartation of spiritual power or gifts by those presiding over the ceremony. Rather, it is an acknowledgement, recognition and confirmation of a personal call, with the presentation of the ministerial charge and prayer for God's enablement. And in Him we are complete, thoroughly furnished unto all good works entire, wanting nothing. He is our ability, the Spirit gives unction to function, therefore, I can do all things through Christ which strengtheneth me.

ORDINATION CEREMONY:

Brethren, these are they whom we propose, God willing, this day to ordain ministers with the Pentecostal Church of God.

Brethren, it is a pleasure to welcome you to the family of hundreds who have stood where you stand tonight.

The call to preach the Word of God is such a high and holy calling that has challenged the hearts of the pioneers of the Pentecostal Church of God, and has been the thrust behind the expansion and advancement of this movement. It is our prayer that your ministry will assist to further this cause to the ends of the earth.

The ceremony of ordination is that in which our movement acknowledges the divine call, the commission and qualifications of a person to

Officiating at Ceremonies

the ministry; extends its blessings, fellowship and opportunities; receives your pledge of dedication, faithfulness and loyalty; and a time when we invoke divine enablement for success in your life and ministry.

You are to study to show yourself approved unto God, to accept the charge given and to walk worthy of your vocation. From this day forward, no excuse as a novice in spiritual experience or service in the ministry, will be acceptable to God. This is your graduation from that state.

EXAMINATION AND QUALIFICATIONS:

The district presbytery has examined your ministry as to:

The genuineness of your Christian experience.

The sufficiency of your spiritual, moral and social maturity.

The reality of your divine call.

The correctness of your doctrine.

The adequacy of your preparation and practical ability.

The acceptability of your allegiance to the policies and programs of the Pentecostal Church of God.

Having thus made this examination they consider you qualified for the rite of ordination, and I will remind you that as long as you exercise your ministry in this district, you are directly amenable to this district board for your conduct and ministry, as well as to God. You are encouraged to build a good record so that you may have a good report from those within and without. Strive always to be an asset to God and the church.

BIBLE PRESENTATION:

Presbyters facing candidates pick up their Bibles and hold together as they repeat:
REPEAT TOGETHER:

I take this Bible of which I am made an interpreter. I will be diligent to study to show myself approved unto God. I take this Word into my heart that I may proclaim it with conviction and power. To the best of my ability and understanding, I will faithfully preach the gospel of Christ. I will myself be an example so that none following me will ever stumble and be lost to the kingdom of God. I will never bring reproach upon this Holy Book. I will seek to be a soul winner and make full proof of my ministry. This I covenant before God and this congregation.

THE CHARGE:

2 Timothy 4:1-5, "I charge thee therefore before God, and the Lord Jesus Christ, who shall judge the quick and the dead at his appearing and his kingdom;

Preach the word; be instant in season, out of season; reprove, rebuke, exhort with all longsuffering and doctrine. For the time will come when they will not endure sound doctrine; but after their own lusts shall they heap to themselves teachers, having itching ears; And they shall turn away their ears from the truth, and shall be turned unto fables. But watch thou in all things, endure afflictions, do the work of an evangelist, make full proof of thy ministry."

I charge you as Paul also charged Timothy of old, "Preach the Word." Your own wisdom is not sufficient, nor is your intelligence or your training.

Officiating at Ceremonies

Your continued and arduous study, you will need always and increasingly, but the ultimate message which you must build into the lives of men and the community must be larger than any wisdom of your own. I charge you, therefore, that by all diligence and by every means, you seek to ascertain the will and Word of God, and translate it into terms that men can grasp for daily living and for eternal measurements. I charge you to be an example unto believers in the Word, in daily living, in charity, in spirit, in faith, in purity. A minister has as many rights as any human but more responsibilities than most men. A true servant of Christ will waive his rights in order to wield an influence for good.

I charge you to remember the word of the Lord Jesus when He said, "He that would lose his life for my sake shall find it" and "He that would be greatest among you, let him be servant of all."

We remind you that from this day forward there is no turning back from the choice you have made and the way you have chosen. You have covenanted with God, your hands have gripped the gospel plow and we charge you never to turn back regardless of the high cost of your ministry.

KNEEL FOR THE PRAYER OF ORDINATION:

(Wives behind their husbands. A song while kneeling.)

IN STANDING POSITION WITH COMPANIONS:

Brethren, we cannot tell what the future holds except for that which God's Word reveals, we cannot promise you an easy way. However, we can prom-

Administrative Resource Manual

ise you that He who has called you to preach shall supply all your need according to His riches in glory. And that He will open a door of effectuality for your ministry according to your preparation and dedication to that ministry.

And when the Chief Shepherd shall appear, you shall receive a crown of glory that fadeth not away and you will hear Him say, "Well done thou good and faithful servant. Enter thou into the joys of thy Lord." This will be sufficient pay for all your labors and it includes dividends.

CHORUS: "It will be worth it all."

Our prayers are with you that you shall be strengthened when you are weak, guided when the way is not clear and that Christ will be your companion when you are lonely.

You are God's servant, ordained to the office of the ministry by the laying on of hands and prayer.

"The Lord bless thee, and keep thee: The Lord make his face to shine upon thee, and be gracious unto thee: The Lord lift up his countenance upon thee, and give thee peace" (Numbers 6:24-27).

"Now the God of peace, that brought again from the dead our Lord Jesus, that great shepherd of the sheep, through the blood of the everlasting covenant, Make you perfect in every good work to do his will, working in you that which is wellpleasing in his sight, through Jesus Christ; to whom be glory for ever and ever. Amen" (Hebrews 13:20, 21).

CERTIFICATE PRESENTATION:

On behalf of the General Executive Credentials Committee and the district board, it gives me great

Officiating at Ceremonies

pleasure to present to you this certificate of ordination with the Pentecostal Church of God.

We pledge you the fellowship of our ministers, our churches and districts, and assure you of our prayers for your ministry.

May God anoint you for service and make your ministry fruitful in every way. God bless you.

Quotes from: *Theological and Functional Dimensions of Ordination*, Gospel Publishing House; *Special Occasion Helps*, C. M. O'Guin, Baker Book House.

CEREMONIES OF DEDICATIONS
CHURCH DEDICATION CEREMONY:

Greetings to all in the name of our Lord who is able to do exceedingly, abundantly, above all that we ask or think, according to the power that worketh in us. Unto him be glory in the church by Christ Jesus throughout all ages, world without end, Amen.

On this auspicious occasion we come to dedicate this fine facility to the glory of God and the worship of His name and the instruction of His Word.

On this special day we commend all those who are responsible for the completion of this project: the leaders and the faithful people who participated. We recognize the many sacrifices of each one and the miracles that God has performed to bring this project to completion.

Therefore, as with Nehemiah, it is a day of great joy. These facilities are a center for evangelism.

DEDICATION MESSAGE:
THE CEREMONY: (pastor and leaders at front)
TO DEDICATE MEANS:

Administrative Resource Manual

To consecrate, to set apart for a special purpose, to devote to special work and duty, to open formally. A public announcement, "We are open for business."

Dedicate is to set apart objects for God's use: Moses' Tabernacle,,Solomon's Temple, Nehemiah's Wall, Private Dwellings, Vessels for Worship, Babies and People.

SCRIPTURE READING:

Portions from Isaiah 66,1 Kings 6, 1 Kings 8, 2 Chronicles 6, Ephesians 2. "Thus saith the Lord, The heaven is my footstool: where is the house that ye build unto me? and where is the place of my rest?

"For all those things hath mine hand made, and all those things have been, saith the Lord: but to this man will I look, even to him that is poor and of a contrite spirit, and trembleth at my word."

"In the four hundred and eightieth year after the children of Israel were come out of the land of Egypt, in the fourth year of Solomon's reign . . . the word of the Lord came to Solomon, saying, Concerning this house which thou art building, if thou wilt walk in my statutes and execute my judgments and keep all my commandments to walk in them; then will I perform my word with thee . . . and will not forsake my people Israel . . . So Solomon built the house, and finished it."

"Then Solomon assembled the elders of Israel, and all the heads of the tribes, the chief of the fathers of Israel . . . and stood before the altar of the Lord in the presence of all the congregation of Israel, and spread forth his hands toward heaven:

Officiating at Ceremonies

And he said, Lord God of Israel, there is no God like thee, in heaven above, or on earth beneath, who keepest covenant and mercy with thy servants that walk before thee with all their heart . . . thou spakest also with thy mouth, and hast fulfilled it with thine hand, as it is this day . . . But will God indeed dwell on the earth? behold, the heaven and the heaven of heavens cannot contain thee; how much less this house that I have builded? Yet have thou respect unto the prayer of thy servant, and to his supplication . . . which thy servant prayeth before thee to day: That thine eyes may be open toward this house night and day even toward the place of which thou has said, My name shall be there . . . And hearken thou to the supplication of thy servant . . . when they shall pray toward this place: and hear thou in heaven . . . and when thou hearest, forgive."

"Now therefore ye are no more strangers and foreigners, but fellow citizens with the saints, and of the household of God; And are built upon the foundation of the apostles and prophets, Jesus Christ himself being the chief corner stone; In whom all the building fitly framed together groweth unto an holy temple in the Lord: In whom ye also are builded together for an habitation of God through the Spirit."

A WORD TO LEADERS AT FRONT:

Think of these officers as Gideon's band, who stood every man in his place. (When officers are in place, have the congregation stand.)

THE ACT OF DEDICATION:

MINISTER: Dearly beloved brethren: Forasmuch as it pleased Almighty God to put it into the heart of His servants to build this house for His worship, let us now fulfill the godly purpose for which we are assembled of dedicating it to the honor of God's most holy name. To the glory of God the Father, who has called us by His grace; to honor of His Son, who loved us and gave Himself for us; to the praise of the Holy Spirit, who illumines and sanctifies us;

PEOPLE: We dedicate this house. For the worship of God in praise and prayer,

MINISTER: For the preaching of the everlasting gospel, For the celebration of the holy communion,

PEOPLE: We dedicate this house.

MINISTER: For the comfort of all who mourn, For strength of those who are tempted, For light to those who seek the way,

PEOPLE: We dedicate this house.

MINISTER: For the hallowing of family life, For teaching and guiding the young, For the perfecting of the saints,

PEOPLE: We dedicate this house.

MINISTER: For the conversion of sinners, For the promotion of righteousness, For the extension of the kingdom of God,

PEOPLE: We dedicate this house.

MINISTER: In loving memory of those who have gone from us, whose hearts and hands have served in this church; with gratitude for all whose faith and consecrated gifts make this house possible; in gratitude for the labors of all those who love and serve this church and

Officiating at Ceremonies

with prayers for all who shall worship in this house in years to come,

PEOPLE: We dedicate this house.

MINISTER: And now, as a people within the household of God, in the unity of faith, in the communion of saints, in love and good will to all, in gratitude for the gift of this house to be an habitation of God through the Spirit.

PEOPLE: We dedicate ourselves to Christ, to the worship of God, and the service of His kingdom, for the ministry of the open Bible, in the name of the Father, and of the Son, and of the Holy Spirit. AMEN.

PRAYER OF DEDICATION:

PRESENTATION OF THE KEYS:
Pastor_____, on behalf of this church and all who have so unselfishly given their time, talents and finances that it may be possible, I want to present to you, as Pastor of the church, the keys to this church. May these doors ever be open to any person who may have a need from the Lord Jesus Christ, no matter what his rank or station in life, no matter how serious his problem, for we want to go to heaven with every person. God bless you and supply your every need by His riches in glory.

DECLARATION OF DEDICATION:
In the name of the Father, and of the Son, and of the Holy Ghost, I now declare this house and these facilities to be forever set apart from all profane and common usages, and consecrated to the worship and service of Almighty God; to whom be glory

and majesty, dominion and power, forever and ever. AMEN.

CLOSING SONG AND CONGRATULATIONS: Suggested song: "Praise the Lord."

Other ceremonies and dedications such as church related buildings, babies, weddings—including 25th and 50th anniversary repeating of vows, ground-breakings, communion, funerals and many others can be found in manuals for ministers which we include in the bibliography.

- SECTION THREE -
MINISTERIAL CREDENTIALS

This section identifies the environment of the minister and the steps in processing a ministerial credential application.

The Minister's Study Series is listed and the necessary applications and forms are included.

In the Pentecostal Church of God the ministry is highlighted as being important as any part of God's work. We are examples and pacesetters of spiritual growth and insight. Therefore we cannot over-emphasize the importance of better qualifying our ministry.

St. Peter's admonition to ministers: "As every man hath received the gift, even so minister the same one to another, as good stewards of the manifold grace of God. If any man speak, let him speak as the oracles of God; if any man minister, let him do it as of the ability which God giveth: that God in all things may be glorified through Jesus Christ, to whom be praise and dominion for ever and ever. Amen" (1 Peter 4:10, 11).

Here he lists a four-fold outline of the ministry:

1. The gift of the ministry.
2. The stewardship of the ministry.

Administrative Resource Manual

3. The oracle to minister.
4. The ability to minister.

The following chapters are included:

Chapter 13 - Identification
Chapter 14 - Processing Credentials
Chapter 15 - Minister's Insurance Plan
Chapter 16 - Minister's Study Series
Chapter 17 - Applications and Related Forms

CHAPTER 13
Identification

Ministerial credentials are a very important element of the minister's life and work. Procedure to process and monitor credential experience is a very important function of the district office. The district secretary normally handles the reporting and records of ministers working with the General Office. However, it is wise for the district superintendent to be equally informed and knowledgeable of the status of ministers within the district and to be capable of reading the computer reports.

The General and District Constitution and Bylaws give important criteria concerning ministerial credentials that must be met in qualifying ministers for credentials. In addition to the bylaw provisions, there is General Board policy to consider.

Always bear in mind that the General Credentials Committee makes its decisions on applicants in keeping with General Bylaws and General Board policy. Therefore, if the district follows this same rule, it can expedite time in processing.

Administrative Resource Manual

If your district feels you are in keeping with by-law and General Board policy provisions and the Executive Committee does not approve your application, you may appeal the decision to the General Board. However, this is seldom done.

The credentialed minister is identified with the leadership and heart of the movement. He contributes his resources to the purpose and objectives as a vital member. As we stay close to the qualifications for approving applications, we have a higher percentage of dedicated and qualified ministers. Our growth must be qualitative as well as quantitative.

It is our goal to see a greater percentage of our ministers become active and full time in the ministry. It does not serve our purpose to license a great number of ministers who remain inactive. Indeed the bylaws provide that an exhorter must meet his district board after two years either for advancement or, should he fail to provide evidence of working toward an active status, his credentials could be terminated. Before an application for advancement to ordination can be considered, the applicant must be in active ministry, giving evidence that he plans to continue in such active ministry.

As a rule, active is defined as a pastor, full-time evangelist, an appointed or elected active position of assistant pastor, Bible college teacher, missionary or church executive position.

As a God-called minister, we are identified with a select, chosen, gifted, totally committed and dedicated group who have given all to follow the Master as classic examples in church leadership and ministry—true disciples of Christ.

The organization is the fellowship group that blends the gifts and abilities of its many members and ministers together to accomplish its God-given

Identification

purpose. As ministers, we are to look to God for open doors of ministry. Brethren and churches respond to the gifts of ministers as they move among the main stream of activity in the movement. "A man's gift maketh room for him, and bringeth him before great men" (Proverbs 18:16).

Loyalty must be stressed to our ministers—not a blind loyalty, of course. If a minister should find himself out of harmony with the organization and its doctrine and practices, it is ethical for him to sever his relations and seek a field elsewhere. It is unethical for him to remain either to bring disharmony among the brethren or to be instrumental in withdrawing a congregation from fellowship, much less to conspire to confiscate a piece of property dedicated to this ministry.

Just as the minister has an ethical responsibility toward his organization, it is only reasonable to believe that his organization has certain responsibilities and obligations toward him. There should be a two-way communication, respect and love in every fellowship. We all contribute to the greatness and effectiveness of the movement.

CHAPTER 14
Processing Credentials

APPLICATIONS:

It is usually the duty of the district secretary and the sectional presbyters to make credential applications with the Pentecostal Church of God available to any minister who should request them. We have credential application forms for new applicants, promotion and reinstatement.

These applications, along with all the necessary supporting documents, should be completed and returned to the district secretary by the specified date. He will prepare the application for presentation to the district credential committee for their decision.

PROCESSING AN APPLICATION FOR MINISTERIAL CREDENTIALS FOR NEW APPLICANTS ONLY:

Before the application is considered by the district credential committee, the district secretary should check to make sure that:

1. All the questions on the application have been correctly answered. Never examine an appli-

Processing Credentials

cant, approve him or pass his application on to the General Credential Committee when his file is incomplete. Applications which are incomplete or answered incorrectly will be returned to the district with a cover letter itemizing the areas that need attention, before consideration by the General Credential Committee.

2. A credential fee payment accompanies the application. The minimum amount is one month's payment; however, some districts require as much as three months' payment.

3. The credential insurance card has been completed, including the date and signature of the applicant.

4. All necessary supporting documents are attached to the application (such as letters of recommendation, marriage questionnaires, substantiation letters, bankruptcy questionnaires, felony questionnaires, etc.).

5. The application has been signed by the applicant.

6. The application bears the signatures of the proper Pentecostal Church of God ministers who are introducing or recommending the applicant for credentials.

STEP BY STEP THROUGH THE APPLICATION:

1. The minister's account number is located in the upper right hand corner. This number will remain the same even if he transfers to another district.

2. The date, full name, gender, address, city, state, zip code, telephone number, social security number, date and place of birth, date and place of conversion, should all be completed.

Administrative Resource Manual

3. Marital status: the appropriate answer should be checked. If married, the next three questions are applicable. If married, give date and place of marriage. If married, give full name of spouse. If married, is spouse credentialed with Pentecostal Church of God? If so, give his/her account number.

4. Have you been divorced? How many times? Has your spouse been divorced? How many times? If single, this question must be answered with a no; N/A or unanswered are not acceptable. Be sure there is a marriage questionnaire (in duplicate) for each divorce of either party. There are printed substantiation letter forms to be completed and mailed by the district secretary to each of the individuals listed on the marriage questionnaire. We request three substantiation letters for each questionnaire. These should be received and placed in the applicant's records before consideration by the district credential committee. If you must wait until the next district meeting to complete these records, then do so. If the applicant's divorce was prior to first experience of salvation, a marriage questionnaire is required, although substantiation letters are not necessary. If the divorce occurred when an unbeliever (one without faith) departed from a believer (1 Corinthians 7:15), the applicant must provide the following:

    a. Divorce decree naming the deserting spouse as the plaintiff, except in the case of extreme extenuating circumstances.

    b. Supporting statements from at least one pastor and/or marriage counselor that counseled with applicant prior to the final decree of divorce.

    c. Substantiation letters from two or three sources which confirm that the spouse of the

Processing Credentials

applicant was the offending party and that the applicant attempted genuine biblical reconciliation.

    1. Expressed a genuine willingness to forgive their spouse.

    2. Made themselves fully accessible to their offending spouse for reconciliation even after the final decree of divorce.

  d. A written statement from the applicant outlining his/her biblical view of divorce and underlying scriptural authority upon which this action has been based.

  e. If at all possible, a statement from the offending spouse.

5. Credentials for which are you applying? Check one. Credentials you now hold? Check one, if applicable.

6. Have you held credentials with any other organization? If answer is yes, give the name of the organization and your reason for leaving. If the applicant has held credentials (within the last five years) with any other organization holding membership with the Pentecostal Charismatic Churches of North America, a letter of reference from that organization is required. If a response is not received within thirty (30) days, the application may be processed without the letter. However, it should be noted on the application, or in an attached letter, that at least thirty days has lapsed since formal request was made.

7. Have you applied to any other district of this organization for credentials? If so, what district? What decision was made concerning your application? If applicant has previously held credentials with the Pentecostal Church of God, the application for reinstatement should be used.

8. The applicant should answer as briefly and yet as thoroughly as possible, the question: "What training have you had to qualify you for the ministry?"

9. The next seven yes and no questions (felony, child sexual abuse, bankruptcy, lodge, drugs, perversion and the occult) must always be answered no except the felony and bankruptcy questions. If these are answered yes, the proper form (felony or bankruptcy questionnaire) must be completed and sent in with the application. According to the General Board policy, anyone desiring credentials with the Pentecostal Church of God who is a member of the Masons, will be required to write a letter of withdrawal stating that they will no longer attend the Masonic meetings or pay dues. A copy of the letter of notification to the Masons should be attached to the application for credentials.

10. The two questions concerning the reading of the general and district bylaws must always be answered yes.

11. The next questions dealing with willingness to conform to and abide by the bylaws must be answered yes.

12. The remaining yes and no questions on the back of the application should be answered yes, except, "Can good works alone save a soul from hell?" which of course is no. Also, the last two questions may be answered yes and no. We will consider an applicant for exhorter credentials who has not read the entire Bible. This is, however, a requirement for all license or ordination applicants.

13. The balance of the application dealing with personal ministerial records must be answered.

14. Be sure the applicant has read the final statement and expressed his agreement and commit-

Processing Credentials

ment to it by signing the application.

15. The application must have the signature of the proper Pentecostal Church of God ministers who are introducing or recommending the applicant for credentials.

16. After (or at the time of) the district credential committee meeting, the district portion of the application should be completed by the district secretary or superintendent.

17. Be sure to include your district's name as well as the location of the meeting.

18. Did applicant have credentials with another organization? If the answer is yes, the next two questions should be answered.

19. Did applicant surrender former credentials? Any credentials held with another organization must be surrendered before Pentecostal Church of God credentials can be issued.

20. What score did the applicant make on the credential examination? (A score of 70 or above is necessary.) The General Board established a policy recommending that ministers coming to us from other organizations complete the credential examination (license or ordination).

21. Always check to see if application bears the signature of the district secretary or superintendent.

Administrative Resource Manual

PROCESSING AN APPLICATION FOR PROMOTION:

We now have an application specifically designed to assist the district and general credential committees in determining if the applicant has met the requirements for promotion to the next credential level. This is called application for promotion.

Before the application is considered by the district credential committee, the district secretary should check to make sure that:

1. The application has been completed correctly.
2. The applicant is current (within 30 days) with his credential fee payments.
3. The form Notification of Completion of the Minister's Study Series (I for License or II for Ordination) is either attached to the application or has been previously sent to the General Office to be placed in the minister's file. If the applicant has completed equivalent studies, a transcript or verification should be attached.
4. The applicant has served the required length of time at his present credential level. A minimum of one year as exhorter before advancing to license or a minimum of two years as licensed before advancing to ordination. In addition, the applicant must have fulfilled at least one year of full-time ministry or if working on a secular job, must have at least two (2) years' experience in an acceptable ministry in order to qualify for ordination.

STEP BY STEP THROUGH THE APPLICATION:

1. The date, name, gender, account number, address, city, state, zip code, telephone, and social security number should all be completed.

Processing Credentials

2. Credentials for which you are applying. Check one. Credentials you now hold. Check one.

3. When did you receive the credential you now hold? The date should indicate when the applicant was approved by the district for the credential presently held.

4. Have you read the entire Bible? While a minister may be granted exhorter credentials without having read the entire Bible, no minister can be granted license or ordination without having read all sixty-six (66) books of the Bible. This does not necessarily mean in numerical order or from front to back.

5. Have you completed the Minister's Study Series I or II? In order to advance from exhorters to license, Series I must be completed. To advance from license to ordination, Series II must be completed. If the applicant shows proof of equivalent studies this rule does not apply.

6. Are you in the full-time active ministry? Full-time has been interpreted to include any minister who is serving as pastor, associate or assistant pastor, evangelist, full-time teacher in Christian school or college. The answer to this question should be yes for promotion to ordination.

7. The remaining three questions dealing with the personal ministerial record of the applicant should be answered.

8. Be sure the applicant has read the final statement and expressed his agreement and commitment to it by signing the application.

9. The application must be signed by the proper Pentecostal Church of God ministers who are introducing or recommending the applicant for promotion.

Administrative Resource Manual

10. After (or at the time of) the district credential committee meeting, the district block of the application should be completed by the district secretary or superintendent.

11. Be sure to include your district name, as well as the location of the meeting. Also, check the credential promotion level of the applicant.

12. Did applicant complete the required Minister's Study Series or its equivalency? A notice of completion should accompany the application unless previously sent to the General Office. Equivalency is determined by the district from a transcript of studies furnished by the applicant. The term "equivalent studies" is understood to mean studies involving equivalent subject matter as opposed to equal units of credit.

13. What score did the applicant make on the credential examination? A minimum score of 70 is necessary. If the minister fails to make 70, he/she may take the examination again at a later date arranged with the district secretary or superintendent. In the case of equivalency, the exam is not mandatory.

14. The section, "If applying for promotion to ordination," must be completed if the promotion is for ordination.

15. Always check to see if the application has been signed by the district secretary or superintendent before mailing it to the General Office.

PROCESSING AN APPLICATION FOR REINSTATEMENT:

We now have an application specifically designed to provide the information needed to determine if a minister who has previously held credentials with

Processing Credentials

the Pentecostal Church of God should be reinstated. This is called Application for Reinstatement.

Before the application is considered by the district credentials committee, the district secretary should check to make sure that:

1. The application is completed correctly.
2. The applicant's credential fees were current when his affiliation was terminated. If fees were not current, the amount owed plus at least one month's payment must accompany the application.
3. If the applicant is not applying through the district he previously held credentials with, a letter of clearance from that district must accompany the application.
4. All necessary marriage questionnaires and substantiation letters are attached to the application.

STEP BY STEP THROUGH THE APPLICATION:

1. The date, name, gender, account number, address, city, state, zip code, telephone, social security number, date of birth, place, date and place of conversion should all be completed.
2. Marital status: The appropriate answer should be checked.
3. If married, give full name of spouse.
4. Have you had a marriage change since you last held credentials with the Pentecostal Church of God? If so, explain. If the applicant has been divorced since he/she last held credentials, a marriage questionnaire must be completed for each divorce and submitted with the application along with three required substantiation letters for each marriage questionnaire. If the applicant has been married, or remarried, since he/she last held credentials, we need to know if the present spouse has

Administrative Resource Manual

ever been divorced. If there has been a divorce, marriage questionnaires are needed for each, along with the necessary substantiation letters.

5. Name of the district in which you were a member when affiliation was terminated? Why did you leave the Pentecostal Church of God? These questions make us aware if a letter of clearance is needed (which would be the case if applicant is not applying through the district in which he last held credentials) and if the problem that caused the termination has been solved.

6. Credentials you held when terminated: check one. The General Board has established a policy that our district boards not reinstate or promote credentials at the same time unless interim experience and/or present position warrants it.

7. Type of ministry in which you are presently engaged. Check the appropriate answer.

8. If a pastor, give the name and location of the church.

9. Did you owe any credential fees when your credentials were terminated? If so, have these been paid? If applicant withdrew, or was dropped, with his credential fees in arrears, the full amount owed plus at least one month's credential payment must accompany the application.

10. If the next three yes and no questions (felony, child sexual abuse and bankruptcy) are answered no, nothing further is needed. If the answer to the felony question is yes, the felony questionnaire must be completed.

The General Board has established the policy that anyone who has been convicted of child sexual abuse will be denied credentials.

If the answer to the bankruptcy question is yes, the bankruptcy questionnaire must be completed.

Processing Credentials

11. Have you read, and are you willing to abide by, the current district and general bylaws? The key word here is "current" since he was required to have read both bylaws before receiving credentials previously, although he could presently be in a different district.

12. The next two questions deal with our doctrinal statement and are therefore very important. Do you without reservation, fully subscribe to our doctrinal statement as contained in the General Constitution and Bylaws, and will you practice and publicly proclaim them from the pulpit? If your present viewpoint differs from that of the Pentecostal Church of God, please list and explain.

13. Be sure the applicant has read the final statement and expressed his agreement and commitment to it by signing the application.

14. The application must be signed by the proper Pentecostal Church of God ministers who are introducing or recommending the applicant for reinstatement.

15. After (or at the time of) the district credential committee meeting, the district block of the application should be completed by the district secretary or superintendent.

16. Be sure to include your district name as well as the location of the meeting. Also, include the level of credential the district approved.

17. The question dealing with when and why the applicant was terminated should be answered.

18. Always check to see if it has been signed by the district secretary or superintendent.

Administrative Resource Manual

APPLICATION FOR MINISTERIAL CREDENTIALS

for NEW APPLICANTS ONLY

PENTECOSTAL CHURCH OF GOD
P. O. Box 850, Joplin, Missouri 64802
Phone: (417) 624-7050

FOR GENERAL OFFICE USE
☐ Approved
☐ Denied

Acct# _____

NOTICE TO APPLICANTS: The Constitution of the Pentecostal Church of God specifically states that the Word of God shall be our rule of faith and basis of fellowship; endeavoring to keep the unity of the Spirit, until we come to the unity of the faith. Upon this basis, we invite the fellowship and cooperation of everyone whom God called to labor in His vineyard as pastor, evangelist or licensed preacher, and who is walking worthy of his call. However, in order that we may have a proper record of our files, it will be necessary that you complete this form. Read the following carefully and ANSWER ALL QUESTIONS. In accepting credentials, the applicant affirms without reservation that he understands, and agrees to be governed by, the General Constitution and Bylaws of the Pentecostal Church of God and the constitution and bylaws of the district where membership is maintained.

Date _____
Full Name _____ Sex _____
Address _____ City _____ State _____ Zip _____
Telephone _____ Social Security # _____
Date of Birth _____ Place _____ Date of Conversion _____ Place _____
Marital Status: ☐ Single ☐ Married ☐ Widowed ☐ Divorced ☐ Marriage annulled
   If married, give date of marriage _____ Place _____
   Full name of your spouse: _____
   Is spouse credentialed with the Pentecostal Church of God? ☐ Yes ☐ No Account# _____
Have you been divorced? _____ If yes, how many times? _____ Has your spouse been divorced? _____
If yes, how many times? _____ (If either you or your spouse have been divorced, an additional form, Marriage Questionaire, must be completed IN DUPLICATE for each divorce and submitted, together with appropriate supporting documents, with this application.)
Credentials for which you are now applying: ☐ Ordination ☐ License ☐ Exhorter
Credentials you now hold: ☐ Ordination ☐ License ☐ Exhorter
Have you held credentials with any other organization? ☐ Yes ☐ No
If answer is yes, what was the name of the organization? _____
Why did you leave? _____
Have you applied to any other district of this organization for credentials? ☐ Yes ☐ No
If so, what district? _____
What decision was made concerning your application? _____
What training have you had to qualify you for the ministry to which you have been called? _____

Have you ever been convicted of a felony? ☐ Yes ☐ No
Have you ever been convicted, indicted or under investigation for child sexual abuse and/or any other criminal sexual conduct? ☐ Yes ☐ No
Have you ever filed bankruptcy? ☐ Yes ☐ No
Are you a member of a lodge, a secret order or secret society? ☐ Yes ☐ No
Do you use intoxicating liquors, narcotics, hallucinogens or tobacco? ☐ Yes ☐ No
Do you approve or practice homosexuality or any other form of sexual perversion? ☐ Yes ☐ No
Do you approve or practice any form of the occult? ☐ Yes ☐ No
Have you read the General Constitution and Bylaws? ☐ Yes ☐ No
Have you read this district's constitution and bylaws? ☐ Yes ☐ No
Are you willing to conform to and abide by the same? ☐ Yes ☐ No
Have you read the entire Bible (all 66 books)? ☐ Yes ☐ No
Do you believe all of it? ☐ Yes ☐ No

(Continued on reverse side)

White: General Office Copy/Yellow: District Office Copy

Application for Credential - New Applicant - Side 1

Processing Credentials

Do you accept our doctrinal position on the Trinity of the Godhead?	☐ Yes	☐ No
Have all men sinned?	☐ Yes	☐ No
Is faith in the shed blood of Jesus essential to salvation?	☐ Yes	☐ No
Do you believe that once saved, it is possible to be lost?	☐ Yes	☐ No
Do you preach and practice water baptism according to Matthew 28:19?	☐ Yes	☐ No
Do you believe Matthew 28:19 to be the only method or formula to be biblically valid for water baptism?	☐ Yes	☐ No
Can good works alone save a soul from hell?	☐ Yes	☐ No
Do you believe that speaking in other tongues is the necessary, initial, physical evidence of the Holy Ghost baptism?	☐ Yes	☐ No
Have you received the Holy Ghost baptism according to Acts 2:4 and Acts 10:44-46?	☐ Yes	☐ No
Do you preach and teach the same?	☐ Yes	☐ No
Is the Holy Ghost a divine person?	☐ Yes	☐ No
Is divine healing in the atonement?	☐ Yes	☐ No
Do you preach and practice the same?	☐ Yes	☐ No
Do you believe Jesus will return to rapture His Church before the Great Tribulation?	☐ Yes	☐ No
Will you preach and abide by the Pentecostal Church of God doctrine?	☐ Yes	☐ No
Do you pay tithes?	☐ Yes	☐ No
Will you send tithes regularly in accordance with your district policy?	☐ Yes	☐ No
Will you fully support both your district and general programs?	☐ Yes	☐ No
Are you now carrying a full schedule of duties as pastor, evangelist, teacher, etc?	☐ Yes	☐ No
If yes, do you intend to continue to do so?	☐ Yes	☐ No

What is your present ministerial position? _____

Where? _____ Of what local church (if any) are you a member? _____

How long have you been attending this church? _____

How long have you been in active ministry? _____

How long have you derived your support from the ministry of the gospel? _____

> Any answer on this application that is later proven to be false is considered perjury and will result in the automatic forfeiture of your credential.
>
> Having read the bylaws and all the requirements of this application, I accept and agree to abide by the same. I further authorize you to contact all persons whom you desire to interview and question about facts concerning my application or my private and public life. I further pledge that I will never file suit or cause of action against the Pentecostal Church of God.

_____
(Applicant's Signature)

Recommended or introduced by: (1) _____
(Pastor)

(2) _____

(3) _____
(Presbyter)

To be completed by district

Approved by the Board of the _____ District at a meeting

held at _____ on _____
(Place) (Date)

Approved for: ☐ Ordination ☐ License ☐ Exhorter

Did applicant have credentials with another organization? ☐ Yes ☐ No
(If applicant has held credentials with a PFNA member organization within the last five (5) years a request for a letter of recommendation is required. If a letter is requested and no response is received within thirty (30) days, proceed without it.)

Did applicant surrender former credentials? ☐ Yes ☐ No

What score did the applicant make on the credential examination? _____

Signed _____
District Secretary or Superintendent

Note: An insurance card must be completed and returned with this application

Application for Credential - New Applicant - Side 2

Administrative Resource Manual

APPLICATION FOR REINSTATEMENT
PENTECOSTAL CHURCH OF GOD
P. O. Box 850, Joplin, Missouri 64802
Phone: (417) 624-7050

FOR GENERAL OFFICE USE
❑ Approved
❑ Denied

Date _____
Full Name _____ Sex _____ Account # _____
Address _____ City _____ State _____ Zip _____
Telephone _____ Social Security # _____
Date of Birth _____ Place _____ Date of Conversion _____ Place _____

Marital Status: ❑ Single ❑ Married ❑ Widowed ❑ Divorced ❑ Marriage annulled
If married, give full name of spouse: _____
Have you had a marriage change since you last held credentials with the Pentecostal Church of God? ❑ Yes ❑ No
If yes, what was the change? ❑ Spouse deceased ❑ Divorce(s) How many times? _____ ❑ Marriage(s) How many times? _____
If this is a new marriage, has your spouse been divorced? _____ If yes, how many times? _____
(If either you or your spouse have been divorced, an additional form, Marriage Questionnaire, must be completed IN DUPLICATE for each divorce and submitted, together with appropriate supporting documents, with this application.)
Name of the district in which you were a member when your affiliation terminated _____
Name of the district through which you are now applying for reinstatement _____
Why did you leave the Pentecostal Church of God? _____

Credentials you held when terminated: ❑ Ordination ❑ License ❑ Exhorter
Type of ministry in which you are presently engaged: ❑ Pastor ❑ Evangelist ❑ Other
If a pastor: _____
               (Name of Church)   (Location)
Did you owe any credential fees when your credentials were terminated? .... ❑ Yes ❑ No
If so, have these been paid? .... ❑ Yes ❑ No
Have you ever been convicted of a felony? .... ❑ Yes ❑ No
Have you ever been convicted, indicted or under investigation for child sexual abuse
and/or any other criminal sexual conduct? .... ❑ Yes ❑ No
Have you ever filed bankruptcy? .... ❑ Yes ❑ No
Have you read, and are willing to abide by, the current district and general bylaws? ..... ❑ Yes ❑ No
Do you, without reservation, fully subscribe to the Pentecostal Church of God doctrinal statement as
contained in the General Constitution and Bylaws, and will you practice and proclaim them from
the pulpit? .... ❑ Yes ❑ No
If your present viewpoint DIFFERS from that of the Pentecostal Church of God, please list and explain: _____
_____
_____
_____

Credential Reinstatement Form - Side 1

Processing Credentials

Any answer on this application that is later proven to be false is considered perjury and will result in the automatic forfeiture of your credential.

Having read the bylaws and all the requirements of this application, I accept and agree to abide by the same. I further authorize you to contact all persons whom you desire to interview and question about facts concerning my application or my private and public life. I further pledge that I will never file suit or cause of action against the Pentecostal Church of God.

_____
(Applicant's Signature)

Recommended or introduced by: (1) _____
(Pastor)
(2) _____
(Presbyter)
(3) _____

```
To be completed by district
Approved by the Board of the _____ District at a meeting
held at _____ on _____
         (Place)                    (Date)
Applicant was terminated on _____
                                (Date)
Due to _____
        (Reason)

_____
Signed by Superintendent or Secretary
```

Credential Reinstatement Form - Side 2

REAFFIRMATION OF DOCTRINAL POSITION

By my signature below, I fully reaffirm my belief and adherence to the doctrinal statement of the Pentecostal Church of God in its entirety, as found in the most recent issue of the General Constitution and Bylaws.

Signed_____ Date_____

Doctrinal Reaffirmation Form

Administrative Resource Manual

APPLICATION FOR PROMOTION

PENTECOSTAL CHURCH OF GOD
P. O. Box 850, Joplin, Missouri 64802
Phone: (417) 624-7050

FOR GENERAL OFFICE USE
❑ Approved
❑ Denied

Date _____
Full Name _____ Acct # _____
Address _____ City _____ State _____ Zip _____
Telephone _____ Social Security # _____
Credentials for which you are now applying: ❑ Ordination ❑ License
Credentials you now hold: ❑ License ❑ Exhorter
When did you receive the credential you now hold? ____/____/____
Have you read the entire Bible (all 66 books)? .... ❑ Yes ❑ No
Have you completed the required Minister's Study Series or its equivalency? .... ❑ Yes ❑ No
Are you in the full-time active ministry? .... ❑ Yes ❑ No
Type of ministry in which you are presently engaged: ❑ Pastor ❑ Associate Pastor ❑ Evangelist ❑ Other_____
If a pastor: _____ (Name of Church) _____ (Location)
How long have you been in the full-time active ministry? _____
How long have you derived your support from the ministry? _____

Having read the bylaws and all the requirements of this application, I accept and agree to abide by the same. I further authorize you to contact all persons whom you desire to interview and question about facts concerning my application or my private and public life. I further pledge that I will never file suit or cause of action against the Pentecostal Church of God.

_____
Applicant's Signature

Recommended or introduced by:

_____ (Pastor)

_____ (Presbyter)

_____ (Minister)

To be completed by district

Approved by the Board of the _____ District at a meeting held at _____ (Place) on _____ (Date)
Approved for: ❑ Ordination ❑ License
Did applicant complete the required Minister's Study Series or its equivalency? ❑ Yes ❑ No
What score did the applicant make on the credential examination? _____

IF APPLYING FOR PROMOTION TO ORDINATION, COMPLETE THE FOLLOWING:
When is applicant to be formally ordained? _____
Where is applicant to be formally ordained? _____
Who is to be the presiding officer? _____

_____
(Signed: District Secretary or Superintendent)

White: General Office Copy/Yellow: District Office Copy

Application for Promotion

Processing Credentials

MARRIAGE QUESTIONNAIRE
(Divorce Number _____)

Acct. # _____

Date _____ 19 _____
Full Name _____ Address _____
City and State _____ Zip _____ Date of Birth _____ Place _____
(City, County and State)

Full Name of Previous Companion (Maiden Name) _____
Date of Marriage to Prior Companion _____ Place _____
(City, County and State)

Date of the final decree of Divorce _____ Place _____
(City, County and State)

Date when you were first saved _____ Place _____
(City, County and State)

Was this divorce previous to your first experience of salvation? ☐ Yes ☐ No
    Did your former companion commit fornication or adultery previous to your divorce? ☐ Yes ☐ No
    Upon what legal grounds was divorce obtained? _____
    Were you the ☐ plaintiff or the ☐ defendant in the divorce action?
    If plaintiff, did your companion contest the divorce? ☐ Yes ☐ No
    Did your companion file a cross complaint in the action? ☐ Yes ☐ No
    Who was awarded custody of the minor children, if any? _____
Date and place of your subsequent marriage _____
Is the party to this marriage still your companion? ☐ Yes ☐ No
Were you a minister when your first divorce was secured? ☐ Yes ☐ No
If so, with what denomination were you affiliated? _____
Why did you choose the Pentecostal Church of God with which to now become affiliated? _____

Give one ministerial and two other references who can substantiate the above statements:

Name _____ Address _____
City and State _____ Zip _____
Relationship _____

Name _____ Address _____
City and State _____ Zip _____
Relationship _____

Name _____ Address _____
City and State _____ Zip _____
Relationship _____

Signed _____

Please Note: **This form must be completed in full, in duplicate,** and filed with your application. **If your companion is divorced,** a similar statement must also be filed by your companion. A separate Marriage Questionnaire must be completed for **each** divorce from either the minister and/or spouse.

White: General Office Copy/Yellow: District Office Copy

Marriage Questionaire

Administrative Resource Manual

SUBSTANTIATION LETTER

Date _____

_____ has made application for ministerial credentials with the Pentecostal Church of God and has given us your name as one acquainted with the applicant and one who could possibly substantiate that his/her former companion (or in some cases, his/her spouse's former companion) committed fornication or adultery which led to their divorce. The applicant alleges that the particulars are:

TO BE FILLED IN BY THE DISTRICT

Applicant (or Applicant's present spouse) _____

was married to _____
(Applicant's former companion)

on _____ in _____
   (Date)   (City, County and State)

They were married for _____ years, but due to fornication or adultery on the applicant's former companion's part, they were divorced with the final decree being handed down _____
                                                                                                    (Date)

in _____
   (City, County and State)

TO BE COMPLETED BY THE SUBSTANTIATOR

I, _____, do hereby declare the above statement to be true and correct and fully understand that I may be held personally liable for any statement or answer that is misleading or untrue which is given the Pentecostal Church of God or other parties involved in regard to this application; and do furthermore agree to hold the Pentecostal Church of God harmless and indemnify the Pentecostal Church of God from any claims which may be made against the church as a result of my statement.

Signed _____ Date _____

Relationship to Applicant or Applicant's Spouse: _____

Your prompt response will be very much appreciated, and will be regarded as confidential information. We would appreciate any additional particular information from your own knowledge which might be helpful in our consideration of the application.

Please return to District Office:

Address:

(If you need additional space, please use the reverse side.)

Substantiation Form

Processing Credentials

Use typewriter or press firmly with ball-point pen — No carbon paper necessary.

UNIFORM TRANSFER

Date _____

This is a transfer for _____ Acct. # _____

an _____ minister of the Gospel in good standing, with the _____ District
(Ordained, Licensed or Exhorter)

to the _____ District.

Former Address _____ City _____ State _____ Zip _____

Former Pastorate _____ City _____ State _____ Zip _____

Present Address _____ City _____ State _____ Zip _____

Present Pastorate _____

Financial Record:

Reverend _____ has paid his/her renewal through _____
(month and year)

Minister's tithe record for the past 12 months is as follows:

$_____ $_____ $_____ $_____
$_____ $_____ $_____ $_____
$_____ $_____ $_____ $_____

Ministerial Record:

Minister has held _____ credentials with the Pentecostal Church of God since _____, 19____
(Exhorter, License or Ordained)

Date of birth _____ Married ☐ Yes ☐ No

Minister is cooperative with a District program by attendance at the District meetings, fellowship meetings, and working with officials: ☐ All the time ☐ Most of the time ☐ Sometimes ☐ Seldom

Minister has served in our district as _____
(Pastor, Evangelist, Other)

If pastor: _____
(Name of Church)

Further comments concerning activities _____
_____
_____

NOTE: No transfer can be made unless minister is current with credential fees. The minister's file (or a copy of the same) should be sent along with the white copy of transfer to the district where minister is transferring.

Signed _____
District Superintendent

_____
District Secretary-Treasurer

(This is a confidential report — please complete in QUADRUPLICATE. Send white copy to District Office where minister is transferring, keep yellow copy on file, send pink copy to the General Office and goldenrod copy to minister being transferred.)

Uniform Transfer Form

Administrative Resource Manual

UNIFORM LETTER OF RECOMMENDATION

Date _____

This is a letter of recommendation for _____ Acct. # _____

an _____ minister of the _____ District.
    Ordained, Licensed or Exhorter

Marital Status: ☐ Single ☐ Married

Financial record in this District:

Reverend _____ has paid his/her renewal through _____
                                                                        month/year

Tithe record for the past twelve months:

$ _____ $ _____ $ _____ $ _____

$ _____ $ _____ $ _____ $ _____

$ _____ $ _____ $ _____ $ _____

Ministerial Record:

Type of ministry in which minister was engaged in the district: ☐ Pastor ☐ Evangelist ☐ Other _____

If Pastor: _____
                                Church

Minister was cooperative with the district program by attendance at district meetings, fellowship meetings and working

with officials: ☐ All the time   ☐ Most of the time   ☐ Sometimes   ☐ Seldom

Further Comments: _____
_____
_____
_____

Signed _____
                District Superintendent

Signed _____
              District Secretary-Treasurer

Uniform Letter of Recommendation

Processing Credentials

FINANCIAL TRANSMITTAL

District _____ Report Date _____

	NAME AND ADDRESS	ACCOUNT NUMBER	CHURCH 5% PARTICIPATION	CREDENTIAL PAYMENT	GENERAL BOARD TITHE
1					
2					
3					
4					
5					
6					
7					
8					
9					
10					
11					
12					
13					
14					
15					
16					
	TOTALS				

Financial Transmittal Form

DROPS AND WITHDRAWALS

FOR MINISTERS REMOVED FROM ACTIVE FILE

District ______________________ Report Date ______________

	NAME AND ADDRESS	ACCOUNT NUMBER	DROPPED	WITHDREW	DECEASED	EFFECTIVE DATE
1						
2						
3						
4						
5						
6						
7						
8						
9						
10						
11						
12						
13						
14						
15						
16						
	TOTALS					

Drops and Withdrawal Form

Processing Credentials

ADDRESS CHANGES IN THE _____ DISTRICT

Date _____, 19____

Please send this information each month to the office of the General Secretary, P.O. Box 850, Joplin, Missouri 64801

Name _____ Account Number _____

Ordained _____, Licensed _____, Exhorter _____

Old Address _____
    (street)   (city)   (state)   (Zip)

New Address _____
    (street)   (city)   (state)   (Zip)

Pastor _____, Evangelist _____, Other _____

If Pastor _____
    Church   Address

Name _____ Account Number _____

Ordained _____, Licensed _____, Exhorter _____

Old Address _____
    (street)   (city)   (state)   (Zip)

New Address _____
    (street)   (city)   (state)   (Zip)

Pastor _____, Evangelist _____, Other _____

If Pastor _____
    Church   Address

Name _____ Account Number _____

Ordained _____, Licensed _____, Exhorter _____

Old Address _____
    (street)   (city)   (state)   (Zip)

New Address _____
    (street)   (city)   (state)   (Zip)

Pastor _____, Evangelist _____, Other _____

If Pastor _____
    Church   Address

Name _____ Account Number _____

Ordained _____, Licensed _____, Exhorter _____

Old Address _____
    (street)   (city)   (state)   (Zip)

New Address _____
    (street)   (city)   (state)   (Zip)

Pastor _____, Evangelist _____, Other _____

If Pastor _____
    Church   Address

(over)

Address Change Form (2 sides available)

Administrative Resource Manual

APPLICATION FOR CHURCH CHARTER

Whereas, The _____,
Name of church to be listed on charter

located in the city of _____, county of _____ and state of _____, has in a duly called meeting held this _____ day of _____,
19_____, declared its desire to share in the privileges extended to member churches of the Pentecostal Church of God, and for the purpose of cooperating with other churches of like precious faith by assuming its responsibilities as set forth in the General Constitution and Bylaws of the Pentecostal Church of God, and the Constitution and Bylaws of the _____ District, Therefore we whose names appear on the church membership records as members in good standing, do hereby make application to the General Executive Committee of the Pentecostal Church of God for recognition as a fully affiliated and chartered church with the Pentecostal Church of God (Incorporated) Joplin, Missouri.

Location of Church _____
Street or Rural Route

Mailing Address for Church _____

Church Phone (_____) _____

What was the status of this church prior to this action: Pioneer Work ☐   Independent ☐   Other ☐

Please explain: _____

Is the church owned or rented? _____
If owned, how is it deeded? _____
Name of Pastor: _____ Acct. # _____
Pastor's Address: _____
Name of Secretary: _____
Name of Treasurer: _____
Names of Deacons: _____
_____
_____
_____

Names of Trustees: _____
_____
_____
_____

Name of C.E. Dir. or S.S. Supt.: _____
Name of PYPA President: _____
Women's Ministry President _____
Name of KMF President: _____
Name of SCF President: _____
: _____

Church Membership _____   Attendance Sunday Morning Service _____
Total Constituency _____   Attendance Sunday Night Service _____

(Over)

Church Charter Form - Side 1

Processing Credentials

This church was opened on _____
                                    (Date)
This church was reopened on _____
                                    (Date)
By whose initiative was this church started? _____

Comments: _____
_____

Endorsed by the Pentecostal Church of God

_____ District   _____
                                              Signature of Pastor

_____   _____
Signed by Superintendent or Secretary (Strike out one)   Signature of Church Secretary

_____   _____
              Date   Signature of Presiding Officer

Note: This application form is in triplicate. The General Office and District Office copies are to be sent to the District Office for endorsement. The Local Church copy is to be retained for the permanent records of the church. The District Office will forward the General Office copy to the Office of the General Secretary who shall (after it has been approved by the General Executive Committee) prepare the church charter and send it to the District Office for the proper signatures. The church charter will be presented to the local church by the District Superintendent (or another district official named by the Superintendent) in a special service arranged by the Superintendent with the pastor. Names of the charter members should be listed below.

CHURCH ROSTER ROLL OF MEMBERSHIP

For General Secretary's Office Only:

Date approved by General Executive Committee _____ Church Acct. # _____

Date entered into records _____ By _____

Church Charter Form - Side 2

Administrative Resource Manual

NEW CHURCH OPENED

Another church has been opened in the _____ District.

In accordance with our general bylaws, this church is being reported for tax status purposes. When the church has developed in spiritual maturity and numerical strength (at least ten (10) members), the church will be set in order. After the application for church charter has been approved by the General Executive Committee, the church will be added to the general assessment roll.

Name of church _____

Location of church _____

Mailing address of church _____

City _____ State _____ Zip Code _____

Name of pastor _____ Account # _____

Address of pastor _____ City _____

State _____ Zip Code _____ Phone# _____

Name of secretary _____

Address of secretary _____

This church was opened on (date) _____

Give a brief history of how this church was started and the name of individuals who pioneered this work. If started by a mother church, give the name and address of the mother church

_____
_____
_____

(Use back of this page if you need additional space.)

This is to certify that the aforementioned church has opened in our district. I, therefore, request that it be added to our roster of churches at the general office for tax status purposes.

Date of this report _____   District Superintendent or Secretary _____

- -

For General Secretary's Office Only:

Date entered into records _____ By _____ Church Acct# _____

New Church Opened Form

118

Processing Credentials

CHANGE IN CHURCH STATUS

White Copy to General Office
Yellow Copy to District Office

District _____
Name of Church _____ Acct. # _____
Location of Church _____
Mailing Address for Church _____

CHANGE:
The name of the church has been changed to:
_____

The location of the church has been changed to:
_____

The mailing address of this church has been changed to:
_____

This church has a new pastor:
 Former Pastor _____ Acct. # _____
 New Pastor _____ Acct. # _____
 Address _____

This church was closed _____
                            Date
This church withdrew _____
                            Date
This church was dropped _____
                            Date

REASON:
_____
_____
_____
_____

_____
Signed by Superintendent or Secretary (strike out one)

_____
Date

For General Secretary's Office only:
 Date action implemented _____ Church Acct. # _____
                    By _____

Church Status Change Form

Administrative Resource Manual

White Copy to General Office
Yellow Copy to District Office

CHANGE IN MARITAL STATUS

For General Office Use
☐ Concur
☐ Differ

Date _____

Minister's Full Name _____ Acct # _____
Address _____ City _____ State _____ Zip _____
Telephone _____ Social Security # _____

WHAT HAS CAUSED THIS CHANGE IN MARITAL STATUS?
☐ New Marriage   ☐ Divorce   ☐ Death of Companion   ☐ Other
Please Explain: _____
_____
_____

If a *NEW MARRIAGE* is involved please furnish the following information:
  Date of current marriage _____
  Place of current marriage _____
  Name of spouse (former or maiden name, if female) _____

  Has your spouse ever been divorced? _____ If yes, how many times? _____
                                      (Yes or No)
  A marriage questionnaire and substantiation letters (if necessary) for each divorce should be attached to this form.

If a *DIVORCE* is involved, a marriage questionnaire must be filled out and it, along with three (3) substantiation letters, should be attached to this form.

If the *DEATH* of your companion is involved, please attach two certified (with raised seals) death certificates. The other forms necessary for your insurance claim will be sent to you promptly.
  Date of death _____
  Cause of death _____

Minister's Signature _____   Date _____

To be completed by the district

After considering the particulars of this marriage change, the district board of the _____
District in a duly called meeting held at _____ on
                                              (Place)
_____ took action to recommend to the General Credential Committee that the credentials of
   (Date)

☐ REMAIN IN FORCE   ☐ BE DROPPED

_____
(Signed by Superintendent or Secretary)

A NEW INSURANCE CARD SHOULD BE COMPLETED AND ATTACHED TO THIS FORM

Marital Status Change Form

Processing Credentials

FELONY QUESTIONNAIRE

Name _____

1. Have you been convicted of more than one felony?   Yes _____   No _____
   (If yes, you must complete a seperate questionaire for each conviction)
2. What was the charge for which you were convicted?
   _____
3. What is the date of your conviction? _____
4. Was time served?   Yes _____   No _____   How much? _____
5. When were you released? _____
6. Are you now on probation?   Yes _____   No _____
7. Were you declared guilty of a felony that caused you to be listed on the national registry for your felony?
   Yes _____   No _____
8. Were you saved at the time?   Yes _____   No _____
9. When were you first converted? _____
10. What have you learned from this experience?
    _____
    _____
    _____
    _____
    _____
    _____
    _____

Signed _____   Date _____

Felony Questionnaire

Administrative Resource Manual

BANKRUPTCY QUESTIONNAIRE

Name _____

1. Have you filed for bankruptcy more than once?   Yes _____ No _____
   (If yes, a separate questionnaire should be completed for each bankruptcy filed.)
2. When did you file for this bankruptcy? _____
3. Where was the bankruptcy filed? _____
4. Was this prior to your first experience of salvation?   Yes _____ No _____
5. The bankruptcy was for reasons?   Personal _____   Business _____
6. Under what chapter was the bankruptcy filed? _____
7. Why was the bankruptcy filed? _____
   _____
   _____
   _____
   _____

8. Have you repaid the debts owed at the time of the bankruptcy?   Yes _____ No _____
9. What have you learned from this experience? _____
   _____
   _____
   _____
   _____
   _____
   _____

Signed _____   Date _____

Bankrupty Questionnaire

Processing Credentials

APPLICATION TRANSMITTAL

Please submit original with applications, retain duplicate for your files.

FOR ALL ORDAINED, LICENSED OR EXHORTER MINISTERS

District _____ Report Date _____

LINE NO.	NAME AND ADDRESS	ACCOUNT NUMBER	APPLICANT TYPE (New / Reinstate / Promote)	APPROVED FOR (ORD. / LIC. / EXH.)	AMOUNT PAID AND ENCLOSED
1					
2					
3					
4					
5					
6					
7					
8					
9					
10					
11					
12					
13					
14					
15					
16					
	Totals				

NOTE: Fees—All applications must be accompanied by credential fees. For reinstatement, all past fees must be paid.
Promotions—Before promotions will be approved, all credential fees for the applicant must be current.

Application Transmittal Form

Administrative Resource Manual

PENTECOSTAL CHURCH OF GOD
ANNUAL LOCAL CHURCH REPORT

Name of church _____

Church account number _ _ _ _ _ _ _ _   Church EIN number _ _-_ _ _ _ _ _ _

Church location _____   County _____

Church mailing address _____
                        Street/P. O. Box   City   State   Zip

Church phone number (___) ___-___   Pastor's phone number (___) ___-___

Pastor's name _____

Pastor's address _____
                  Street/P. O. Box   City   State   Zip

How many years has pastor served this church? _____ Is church in full fellowship? (chartered) Yes ___ No ___

OUTREACH

Number saved _____

Number filled with Holy Spirit _____

Number baptized in water _____

Christian day school?   Yes ___ No ___

ATTENDANCE

Average Sunday school attendance _____

Average Sunday morning worship _____

CONSTITUENCY

Church membership _____
Plus
(Non-members who call this their church home) _____

Total constituency _____

PROPERTY

Total value of all church property _____

Total debt of all church property _____

FINANCES

Total annual church income from all sources _____

Signed _____ Date _____
        (Pastor or Church Secretary)

White copy—General Office copy
Yellow copy—District Office copy
Pink copy—Local Church copy

Annual Local Church Report

CHAPTER 15
Minister's Insurance Plan

The 1971 General Convention, sensing the need for a reasonable form of insurance benefits, adopted a uniform program. According to this plan, each minister of the Pentecostal Church of God has life insurance benefits as a part of his/her credential package. The cost of this insurance is included in the monthly credential fees. The plan furnishes a group life insurance program for the minister, together with accidental death and dismemberment benefits. For the minister's dependents, it furnishes group life insurance. A handbook defining the coverage features and general policy information is available to all ministers through the General Office.

It should be clearly noted that any time a minister's credential account gets as much as 90 days in arrears, his insurance is cancelled. Notices to this effect are sent to the minister. To get the insurance reactivated, the account must be brought completely up to date and the minister may be required to complete a form "Evidence of Insurability."

CHAPTER 16
Minister's Study Series

Historically the Minister's Study Series, as a national mandatory program, had its beginning in June 1979, where at the General Convention we considered and adopted a resolution to approve the recommended study series by the General Credentials Committee and General Board.

The title of the study program, Minister's Study Series, was adopted. The theme Scripture is taken from 2 Timothy 2:15, "Study to shew thyself approved unto God, a workman that needeth not to be ashamed, rightly dividing the word of truth."

The program includes Series I for exhorter ministers wishing to advance to license, and Series II for licensed ministers wishing to advance to ordination. The mandatory study program was activated January 1, 1980 and has a five year successful performance qualifying ministers for full-time service.

Therefore, after the six month preparation period was completed, the long-awaited Minister's Study Series was offered for personal study and spiritual enrichment for all new ministers and those advancing to license and ordination. Since the

Minister's Study Series

Minister's Study Series is the mandatory official study course for ministers, a certificate of completion is compulsory for advancing in credential status.

Exceptions to the rule are those who have completed equivalent studies in college or elsewhere. A transcript of studies must accompany the application as substantiation of equivalent studies. Also, a questionnaire test is provided for ministers transferring to us from sister organizations. They must have an acceptable grade or be requested to take certain courses that they may have failed in the test.

The following is a list of the Minister's Study Series:

Series I:
- New Testament Survey
- Old Testament Survey I
- Old Testament Survey II
- Basic Homiletical Studies
- General Constitution and Bylaws
- Basic Bible Truth

Series II:
- Teaching Techniques, Christian Education
- What the Bible Says About the Holy Spirit
- How to Prepare Bible Messages
- Developing the Leader Within You
- Prevision of History/Daniel
- Prevision of History/Revelation

A workbook is published for each study. The minister completes the workbook and sends it to the district office. A district grading officer grades each workbook and signs a completion form.

Administrative Resource Manual

CHAPTER 17
Applications and Related Forms

APPLICATION FOR MINISTERIAL CREDENTIALS FOR NEW APPLICANTS ONLY

All ministers must use this form in their initial application for credentials with the Pentecostal Church of God. It should be carefully read and completed correctly. All questions should be answered satisfactorily and the applicant's signature must appear at the designated place.

The number in the top right hand corner will be the applicant's account number. It will remain the same even if he transfers to another district.

All the supporting documents should accompany the application form when it is sent to the General Secretary's office. At least one month's credential fee along with the orange insurance enrollment information card must accompany each new application. If either the applicant or spouse has been divorced, a marriage questionnaire for each divorce must be attached. If the divorce occurred after the applicant's (or applicant's present companion's) first experience of salvation, three substantiation letters for each divorce are requested. These letters must substantiate fornication or adultery on the part of his/her former companion.

If the applicant has held credentials within the last five years with another PCCNA (Pentecostal Charismatic Churches of North America) organization, a letter of reference from that organization should be attached. If there is no response to the letter after thirty (30) days, proceed without it. However, a note or letter of explanation from the district secretary should be attached.

APPLICATION FOR PROMOTION

This is a new simplified form used by ministers who presently hold exhorter or license credentials and are applying for advancement. Each question, whether applicable to the minister or not, should be answered.

A minister may hold exhorter credentials without having read the entire Bible; however, this is a requirement for promotion to license. Before being promoted from exhorter to license, the minister must have his exhorter credentials for a minimum of one year. He/she must also complete Minister's Study Series I or its equivalency.

For promotion from license to ordination, the minister must have spent at least two years as a licensed minister, completed Minister Study Series II or its equivalency, and be involved in the active ministry. The section dealing with when and where the ordination ceremony will be held must be completed by the district office. This will insure the preparation of the proper certificate and fellowship card.

The application must be signed by the applicant.

APPLICATION FOR REINSTATEMENT

When a minister has previously held credentials with the Pentecostal Church of God and wishes to be reinstated, this form should be used.

Each question should be answered. Some questions are designed to determine if there has been a change in the minister's marriage, doctrine or attitude since last holding credentials. If there has been a divorce, a marriage questionnaire along with the accompanying substantiation letters should be attached. If there has been a remarriage, all the information concerning the applicant's companion should be furnished as with a new applicant.

As a general rule, a minister should be reinstated at the same credential level he held when terminated. A letter of recommendation from the former district is required if he is seeking reinstatement through a district other than the one of which he was a member when his affiliation terminated. This letter should accompany the application.

If the minister owes credential arrears, this must be cleared before the application can be processed.

The application must be signed by the applicant.

MARRIAGE QUESTIONNAIRE

A marriage questionnaire form should be completed for each divorce of either the minister or his spouse. Three substantiation letters should accompany each marriage questionnaire unless the divorce was prior to the minister's or companion's first experience of salvation.

Applications and Related Forms

The purpose of this form is to establish whether or not the divorce and remarriage falls within the General Bylaw provision.

General Bylaws, Article XVIII, page 42:

"No divorced and remarried Christian shall be granted credentials with the Pentecostal Church of God except when such divorce and remarriage occurred prior to the first experience of salvation or was for the cause of fornication (Matthew 5:32)."

Each question on the form should be answered whether it applies to the minister or not.

SUBSTANTIATION LETTER

This form is to be used by the district office when writing to the references listed on the marriage questionnaire. These references should be individuals who can substantiate that the former companion of the minister or his spouse did commit fornication or adultery prior to their divorce.

Three substantiation letters are requested for each marriage questionnaire. Although this form is available, some individuals prefer to write a personal letter. This is acceptable so long as the letter actually substantiates fornication. The letter should, however, be more than a good character reference.

UNIFORM TRANSFER

This form is used to report the transfer of ministerial credentials from one district to another. It should not be used to transfer credentials to another organization.

The transfer form is printed in four parts. The white copy should be sent to the district to which the minister is transferring. The yellow copy should be retained in the district office. The pink copy should be mailed to the General Secretary's office, and the goldenrod copy sent to the person being transferred.

No transfer can be made unless the minister is current with his credential fees. The minister's file (or a copy of the same) should accompany the white copy.

UNIFORM LETTER OF RECOMMENDATION

This form is provided for the convenience of the district office. It is usually given to a minister, upon request, when the minister is planning to be in an area where he is not well known.

FINANCIAL TRANSMITTAL

This green form should be used by the district secretary-treasurer when sending money to the General Office (General Board tithes, credential fees, 5% participation, etc.).

DROPS AND WITHDRAWALS

This blue form is used to supply the General Secretary's office with authorization to drop or withdraw a minister's credentials. This form can also be used to report deceased ministers.

ADDRESS CHANGES

This form is used by the district to supply the General Secretary's office with any change of address or type of ministry for any minister.

SETTING A CHURCH IN ORDER

This form is used by the chairman (district superintendent, presbyter, pastor, etc.) of a church business meeting when a congregation is set in or-

Applications and Related Forms

der and/or wishes to become affiliated with the Pentecostal Church of God. After the form is completed, it should be sent to the General Secretary's office, who in turn takes it to the Executive Committee for approval.

Upon approval, a lovely charter, suitable for framing, is sent to the district office for presentation to the local church.

ANNUAL LOCAL CHURCH REPORT

These forms are provided to each district office in December of each year. They are to be mailed by the district to each local church requesting that they be completed and returned to the district office by the end of January. From these reports the district will compile a summary of the Annual Local Church Reports from their district. The summary along with the white copies from each local church should be mailed to the General Secretary's office by the end of February.

APPLICATION TRANSMITTAL

This form should be completed by the district secretary and mailed along with any applications (new, reinstatement or promotion). The applicant's name, address, account number, type of application, level of credential applied for, as well as the amount of credential fee payment enclosed should be included on the form.

Administrative Resource Manual

- SECTION FOUR -

POLICY AND PROCEDURE

This section of the manual deals with the policies and procedures for the implementation of our work.

In a church function there should not be burdensome or unnecessary length to policy and procedure, but as with organizational structure, policy and procedure should be as simple as possible — yet sufficient to serve the need.

This section contains the following chapters:

Chapter 18 - Policy/Procedure Explained
Chapter 19 - Planning Our Work, Working Our Plan
Chapter 20 - Guide to Parliamentary Procedure

CHAPTER 18
Policy/Procedure Explained

POLICY IS:

One of the most misunderstood and misused tools of management. First let us define policy from Webster's Dictionary and Management Handbook to better understand its concept.

"Policy is a conduct of management, a principle, plan, or cause of action as pursued by an individual or organization.

"Policies are guides to thinking in decision making. Their task is to delimit an area within which a decision may be made and to insure that a decision will contribute to the attainment of objectives and desired plans. Policies are thus a type of plan since they are expected to guide decisions for future action. Too often policies are regarded as 'written on stone,' and the old cliche that 'we do not know why we do it, it is just our policy' is too often true."

In the case of policies, people are expected to think; in the case of rules and procedures, if the

Administrative Resource Manual

rules and procedures are correctly conceived, and applied, people are not expected to think.

Policies furnish the framework for plans. Policies also have the advantage of helping pre-decide issues without repetitive librarians' research.

Policies, usually based on precedents, need to be sufficiently flexible to be adjusted to variation in operations. Their underlying purpose is to induce uniformity in performance.

Seven guidelines for making effective policies:

- Make sure that policies reflect objectives and plans.
- Policies should be consistent.
- Policies should be sharply distinguished from rules and procedures.
- Policies must be looked upon as subject to change.
- Policies should be in writing.
- Policies should be taught.
- Policies should be controlled.

Then, it is wise, in whatever size of organization or function that each member of that constituency be apprised of and clearly understand the policy that he or she is expected to comply with. For as it has been said, "We suffer more ill from a lack of understanding or a misunderstanding than from direct opposition."

PROCEDURE IS:

"The act, method or manner of proceeding in some process or course of action; especially the sequence of steps to be followed; a particular course of action or way of doing something."

Policy/Procedure Explained

Procedures are instructions relative to establish order by which intended end results are more readily realized as one follows the proper sequence.

Some resist procedure and the following of orderly steps for achievement believing procedure to be unnecessary red tape and time consuming, only to experience unsatisfactory or disastrous results.

There is a certain way, a method, and orderly steps to be followed in processing any business or effort to achieve desired results. Most shortcuts short circuit proper procedure and often generate confusion compounding the problem.

Therefore, it is wise to learn the proper course and follow through for best results.

POLICIES, PROCEDURES AND NORMS

Excerpts from the Christian Leadership Letter, January 1980: Relationships are governed within organizations with a variety of rules and regulations which can be thought of as policies, procedures and norms.

Policies are standards against which the organization measures its performance.

Procedures are the methods of working out policies, ways of doing things.

Norms are the standards by which the organization will live out its daily life. They are often unspoken.

Policies, procedures and norms can do much to make an organization operate more effectively and efficiently. Every organization needs a plan that will capture policies and procedures and recognize norms. Increased effectiveness is the result of fewer false starts and fewer mistakes. Policies and procedures are the lessons of history that keep us from reinventing the wheel or forgetting to carry a spare tire. Use them judiciously and with care. Just make sure you make someone responsible (you?) to see that they are recognized, defined and communicated.

Policies

It is quite easy to assume policies. As an organization grows and finds that doing things in a certain way seems to bring the best results, one may hear, "That's our policy!" By the above definition it may or may not be a policy. At the moment it may be just a norm. Somewhere in the growth of the organization one has to decide: 1) what is meant by policy, 2) who will formulate and recommend policy, 3) who will approve policy, 4) how will the policy be made known to those it affects, 5) how will we measure performance against the policy, and 6) how will we go about changing policy?

Procedures

A procedure is a standard way of doing something. It usually proceeds out of experience. Often the experience is gained by mistakes. ("Let's never do that again!") It's often more difficult to write down procedures than it is policy, just as it is easier to tell people what to do than how to do it.

Some procedures fall out quite naturally within the work context: who will use the copying machine and how it will be serviced; how expenses will be reported; what bookkeeping procedures we will use. Other procedures come with much more difficulty.

The key to identifying the need for and writing good procedures is to recognize that they have to do with people. We cannot overstate this. Proce-

Policy/Procedure Explained

dures should be designed with people in mind. People are not machines. People have the wonderful ability of finding better ways of doing things (as well as avoiding ways that they don't like).

Norms

Some norms will be specified as such. Some organizations call them "codes." One can think of such things as dress codes or time and length of coffee breaks. In other words, they are rules which govern our behavior.

Norms tend to grow out of situations. They tend to reflect "The way we do things around here." Often a norm will develop into a policy.

CHAPTER 19
Planning Our Work, Working Our Plan

It is said that, "the wise church leader is not reactive, but proactive. He does not simply react to what happens, but he acts to make things happen."

There are things that exist by design, vision and planning, and things that have evolved. Things planned are manageable for success, others are left to chance and circumstances.

Because of the eternal element connected with church work, and in that souls are at stake, nothing should be left to succeed by existing circumstances. Instead we must plan our work and work our plan to achieve satisfactory and continuing results.

The first law of heaven is order. God is the master planner who performs His work by a design and definite plan so that He knows the end from the beginning. If we are doing His work, it stands to reason that we must proceed on a planned course which He directs.

Planning Our Work, Working Our Plan

DEFINITION OF PLAN:

- "A scheme or program for making, doing, or arranging something."
- "Plan refers to any detailed method, formulated beforehand, for doing or making something."
- "To predetermine a course of action."

DESIGN:

"Design stresses the final outcome of a plan and implies the use of skill or craft in executing or arranging this."

- "Planning therefore, is doing specified work today to cause desired results tomorrow."
- "Planning is making decisions in advance of action."
- "If we could first know where we are, and whether we are tending, we could better judge what to do and how to do it" (Abraham Lincoln).

We have often heard people say, when something does not turn out right, or brings disappointing results; "someone failed to plan." What they were implying is that somewhere back at the beginning there was a lack of foresight by leadership to visualize desired results and lack of effort in establishing definite steps toward achievement, as well as failure to monitor progress (or the lack of it) and to evaluate our direction and course periodically so as to make needed adjustments or changes to bring success.

We can only manage what we plan. We can only reach goals and desired objectives if we control and work the plan. Because we are not all-knowing we may need to adjust the plan occasionally to achieve our purpose.

Administrative Resource Manual

A book has been written titled, *Planagement,* by Robert M. Randolph. The simple idea of this title is how to "move concept into reality."

There must be a plan designed for accomplishment. But to achieve the purpose there must be management along the way toward the goal.

Unfortunately some are stuck on concepts. They are busy planners always drawing plans, but never achieving the results, never moving concept to reality. It is equally important to have people who can take the plan and achieve designed results as it is to draft the plan.

The book mentioned above gives the process that integrates the art and science of converting a concept into reality through the use of a practical method.

The book was designed to serve those individuals and organizations which are committed to constantly improving their present situation while mastering the self-discipline required for present pursuit of excellence and the achievement of potential.

To illustrate, there is an interesting story of an officer delivering supplies to the troops fighting in the Civil War. They came to a river at sundown and camped for the night. Before retiring the officer urged his engineers to devise a method to cross the river. The wranglers, blacksmiths and others who performed various services and odd jobs for the unit overheard the officer urging the engineers as to the importance of getting the supplies to the troops to win the war.

Early the next morning the company officer awoke, stepped out of his tent and much to his surprise there was a bridge across the river. A crude construction, but nevertheless a bridge. The officer was so filled with joy that he said, "Where are my

Planning Our Work, Working Our Plan

engineers? I would like to congratulate them." One of the blacksmiths standing by said, "Sir your engineers are over there in the tent drawing pictures on how to build a bridge. But we felt the urgency as you spoke last night of getting the supplies through, so we worked all through the night, and sir, there is your bridge."

Plan we must, but achievement and results are what counts. We do reach satisfying conclusions as we plan our work and work our plan.

We must learn that the dream and the reality of significant undertakings are indivisible. A dream is not viable without muscle, e.g., processes, procedures, systems and policies, which are the ways to measure from the beginning of concept the accomplishment of the desired end result.

Materials, such as the book *Planagement*, detail a plan for planning. Our interest here is to emphasize the importance of planning. Success in our work, as with any work, depends largely on planning our work and working our plan.

JAWBREAKING AND MINDBENDING

"An individual or organization that does not plan and manage the future may not have one" (Robert M. Randolph).

Lack of proper planning puts individuals and organizations on the defensive instead of the offense. People get caught in the trap of reacting to crises rather than implementing preplanned actions, thus they spend most of their time fighting fires. By contrast, we read in Scripture, "Any enterprise is built by wise planning, becomes strong through common sense, and profits wonderfully by keeping abreast of the facts" (Proverbs 24:3, 4, LB).

Administrative Resource Manual

The starting point to planning is to realize two truths:
- God has a plan for you.
- God is the source of power to achieve plans.

A Christian leader must realize his job is to determine the action God wants him to take and then trust God for the results. As the Bible says, many are the plans in a man's heart, but it is the Lord's purpose that prevails (Proverbs 19:21).

Truly in his heart a man plans his course, but the Lord determines his steps (Proverbs 16:9). There the Christian leader must first recognize God has a plan and prayerfully seek it. Once the plans are formalized and executed, he must trust God for the results.

Here are six stages in the planning process, taken from *Management: A Biblical Approach*, by Myron Rush.

Stage One
Identify the purpose of the project or activity.
1. The purpose tells why the plan is important.
2. The purpose develops conviction and commitment to the plan.

Stage Two
Visualize the plan completed.
1. Visualizing the plan completed builds confidence and faith in the project and purpose.
2. It speeds up the planning process.

Stage Three
Develop measurable objectives.
1. Objectives tell what will be accomplished.
2. Objectives tell how much will be achieved and when.

Stage Four
Identify the activities needed to accomplish the objectives.

Planning Our Work, Working Our Plan

1. Activities explain how the objectives will be achieved.

2. This phase of the planning process should focus on participation, innovation and creativity.

Stage Five

Place the activities in proper sequence.

1. This stage explains where each activity fits in the overall plan.

Stage Six

Determine the resources needed to achieve the plan.

1. When considering resources needed, one must look at people, space, equipment, supplies, time and money.

2. The amount of resources needed will depend on the activities to be performed and their sequence.

Consensus: Purpose — why
Objectives — what, when
Activities — how

From this point let us proceed on the planned course, working the plan, remaining open to evaluation and making adjustments when needed.

Remember, in this world our one remaining constant is *change*.

Question, "Is our work important enough to plan it?"

CHAPTER 20
Guide to Parliamentary Procedure

The following guide to parliamentary procedure points of interest includes quotes from the following resources:

- *Robert's Rules of Order Newly Revised*
- *A Primer of Parliamentary Law*
- *Parliamentary Procedure* published by the National Association of Parliamentarians
- *General Constitution and Bylaws* of the Pentecostal Church of God

Parliamentary procedure was devised to help, not hinder, decision making. It is essentially a logical approach for working together in groups. Its purpose is to provide an orderly and effective means to facilitate the conducting of business. Proper regard for all must be insured: the majority must prevail; the minority must be heard; and the rights of the individual members must be protected. Parliamentary procedure is simply common sense used in a gracious manner.

PRINCIPLES OF PROCEDURE

There are several fundamental (basic) principles that should be noted in the study of parliamentary procedure.

ONLY ONE SUBJECT AT A TIME may be before the assembly. Only one person at a time should have the floor to speak.

EACH MEMBER HAS EQUAL RIGHTS. Each member has an equal right to speak, make motions, participate in debate, vote and hold office (according to the rules established by the organization).

THE FULL AND FREE DEBATE principle is designed to give those who so desire the opportunity to voice their views either for or against the motion. No motion should be voted on until opportunity has been given for both sides of the question to be thoroughly discussed. Unless the rules of order provide otherwise (which is the case with our General and district conventions) each member is entitled to speak twice the same day on the same motion. He should not exceed ten minutes for each time he speaks. It should be noted, however, that each member should have the right to debate once before any previous speaker can claim the floor a second time.

THE ORGANIZATION IS PARAMOUNT. The wishes of the organization supersede those of any individual or group of individuals. Each individual should be concerned about the organization as a whole rather than any personal advantage.

THE MOTION OR ISSUE IS THE ITEM UNDER DISCUSSION, never the person who made the motion. No personalities should be indulged in.

NO QUESTION ONCE SETTLED MAY BE PRESENTED AGAIN in the same form in the same session. It can be brought back for discussion only through a motion to reconsider.

A MAJORITY VOTE DECIDES what an organization wishes to do, except in cases where the basic rights of members are involved, then a larger vote is required.

As a rule of thumb, **A TWO-THIRDS VOTE IS NECESSARY** when any motion deprives a member of his rights in any way.

SILENCE GIVES CONSENT. When a member does not vote, by his silence he agrees to accept the decision of the majority.

"Fundamentally, under the rules of parliamentary law, a deliberative body is a free agent - free to do what it wants to do with the greatest measure of protection to itself and of consideration for the rights of its members." — Robert's Rules of Order Newly Revised, page xlii.

RULES GOVERNING BUSINESS

The various rules which an organization may formally adopt are:

CORPORATE CHARTER OR ARTICLES OF INCORPORATION. This is a legal instrument which contains the name, purpose and other information required by the state in which the organization is incorporated. Incorporation is necessary if an organization owns property or makes contracts. The Articles of Incorporation should be drafted by an attorney familiar with the laws of the state in which the organization is located.

CONSTITUTION AND/OR BYLAWS. Formerly the basic rules of an organization were divided into two documents, the constitution and the bylaws.

In this case the constitution was more difficult to amend than the bylaws. It is now recommended by Robert's Rules of Order Newly Revised that all of an organization's rules be combined into a single instrument, usually called the "bylaws," "constitution" or "constitution and bylaws." Bylaws cannot be suspended unless they contain a specific provision for suspension.

STANDING RULES AND/OR SPECIAL RULES OF ORDER. As practiced in the Pentecostal Church of God, standing rules and special rules of order are synonymous.

RECOMMENDED STANDING RULES OF ORDER FOR THE DISTRICT CONVENTION

All business of the convention shall be governed by accepted rules of parliamentary procedure in keeping with the spirit of Christian love and fellowship. The current edition of Robert's Rules of Order shall serve as a reference text. However, in order to facilitate and expedite the business of the convention, we submit the following rules of order:

Delegation:

The voting constituency shall consist of all officers of the district; ordained and licensed ministers, those licensed to exhort and their companions who have an experience of salvation, and are registered; all accredited missionaries; one (1) representative or delegate per one hundred (100) membership, or fraction thereof, from each affiliated (charter) church. All the voting constituency shall be present and registered, and shall show proper credentials to the Credential Committee, who shall pass on whether or not they shall be seated.

Administrative Resource Manual

Seating the Constituency:

The voting constituency shall be properly seated and counted (other than hearing various reports) before the business session begins, and shall occupy those seat rows designated by the chairman.

Parliamentarians and Timekeeper:

The chair shall appoint a committee of three (3) members who shall serve as parliamentarians. This committee shall decide any question that arises relative to parliamentary procedure.

Discussion:

All resolutions shall be processed by the Resolutions Committee before presentation. No resolution shall be received by the committee after the day and times established and announced by the committee.

No motion from the floor shall be entertained that proposes to amend the Constitution and By-laws which has not been processed by the Resolutions Committee.

Persons desiring to speak shall first rise, address the chair and wait to be recognized. No person shall speak more than three (3) times on any given item of business, and shall speak only on the subject under discussion. The speaker shall be limited to three (3) minutes the first time; two (2) minutes the second; and one (1) minute the third time. In case of two or more persons desiring recognition at the same time, the chair shall recognize the one farthest from the chair. No one is entitled to the floor a second time in debate on the same motion as long as there are other members who have not spoken on the subject and desire the floor.

Debate on any one specific item shall be limited to one (1) hour and the chair shall call for the question at the end of that allotted time.

Guide to Parliamentary Procedure

Recognizing the rights of others to their opinions, we request that no personalities shall be indulged in from the floor. The chairman shall enforce the ruling which states that speakers shall speak only on the subject under discussion.

Because sufficient time is allotted to all those desiring to speak we request that no audible expressions such as "Amen, that's right," etc., be permitted while another is speaking. And, no person shall request the floor while another is speaking except to raise a privileged question.

Each speaker shall, when discussing any subject, state whether he is for or against the issue being presented. When as many as three persons have spoken in succession on the same side of the question being debated, the fourth person must speak on the other side of the question. If there is no speaker for the other side, the chair shall call for the question.

The author of any resolution or recommendation shall be extended an opportunity by the chairman to speak first in explanation of his legislation as to its intent before debate begins. The allotted time shall be three (3) minutes.

The chair shall determine when the discussion is sufficient and the question is to be entertained.

Voting:

All officers shall be elected by two-thirds (2/3) of the votes cast. All officers shall be voted upon by secret ballot.

Any issue, other than balloting for the election of officers, may be voted upon by secret ballot at the request of any member of the voting constituency.

In the election of officers not more than ten (10) ballots (including nominating ballots) shall be cast upon any group of nominees. In the event that no election has been reached by the tenth ballot the nominations shall be reopened and new ballots cast.

The first three (3) ballots shall be nominating ballots. After three ballots have been cast and no election reached, only the two (2) highest names will be voted upon. Any votes for those other than the two highest shall not be counted in the total votes cast. In case one nominee of the two highest being considered should withdraw his name after the first electoral ballot, leaving one nominee for consideration, he shall be accorded a yes or no ballot. Otherwise no office shall be filled by a yes or no vote. Blank ballots shall not be honored and shall not be recognized in computing any totals.

Inasmuch as the voting constituency of some conventions is so large that much time would be required in counting ballots for the election of officers and other items that may be decided by secret ballot, the chairman of the convention shall use tellers and ushers to count the ballots secretly and quickly in an adjoining area, then report their findings to the chairman and he to the convention.

Additionally:

All matters coming before the district convention shall be decided by majority vote except those requiring a two-thirds (2/3) vote, as set forth in the district constitution and bylaws. In order to expedite time for business, after the tenth resolution is processed, we shall begin the election of officers, continuing to process resolutions while ballots are being counted.

PARLIAMENTARY AUTHORITY. Although the basic points of parliamentary procedure are universally accepted, there are some minor differences

Guide to Parliamentary Procedure

in interpretation. For this reason most organizations designate a particular authority to whom all questions concerning procedure are referred. By far the most commonly accepted authority in the United States is Robert's Rules of Order Newly Revised.

If adopted as a resolution by the convention, the recommended rules of order should be printed in the district bylaws.

STEPS IN PRESENTING A MOTION

There are eight steps necessary in order to obtain action on a main motion in a meeting. They are:

1. Obtaining the floor. The member with a motion, stands and addresses the chair, "Mister (or Madam) Chairman."

2. Assigning the floor. The chair recognizes the member he saw stand first (if standing rules do not specify otherwise) and assigns him the floor by calling his name (if known) or nodding to him.

3. Stating the motion. The member who has been assigned the floor now introduces his motion by saying, "I move that . . ."

4. Seconding the motion. Another member (at least two members must be interested in the motion in order for it to be worthy of the time required for consideration) without standing, says, "I second the motion."

5. Stating the motion. The chair states the motion in the same words used by the proposer. "It has been moved and seconded that . . ." To use a different wording the chair must have the consent of the proposer. After it has been stated by the chair the motion becomes the property of the assembly, and the proposer cannot modify it without the consent of the assembly.

Administrative Resource Manual

6. Debating the motion. The chair opens the discussion for full debate by saying: "Are there any questions?" - "Is there any discussion?" Unless the rules of order specify otherwise, each member is allowed one ten-minute debate before a member is allowed a second chance to debate. The mover of the motion should be granted the privilege of opening and closing the debate. Good debate calls for both sides of the proposition to be discussed.

7. Voting on the motion. The chair then takes the vote by saying: "The question is on the motion that . . . (repeating the motion). Those in favor will say 'Aye'. Those opposed will say 'No'." The affirmative vote is always taken first. Likewise a motion should always be stated in the positive. After the affirmative vote the negative vote must always be taken.

8. Announcing the result. The chair announces the result of the vote by stating: "The 'Ayes' have it, the motion is carried, and . . . (repeats the content of the motion)." Or "The 'Nos' have it, the motion is lost, and . . . (repeats the content of the motion in the negative)." The action is never complete until the chair has announced the result of the vote.

CLASSIFICATION OF MOTIONS. Motions may be grouped in five classifications: privileged motions, subsidiary motions, the main motion, incidental motions and motions that bring a question before the assembly again.

THE MAIN MOTION OR RESOLUTION

The purpose of the main motion is to introduce a particular matter to the assembly for its consideration and action. After the motion has been stated by the chair, it is called the question.

Guide to Parliame...

There are two kinds of main mot... and incidental. The original main m... to bring a new subject before the assem... dental main motion is only incidental t... ness of the assembly. Examples of incid... tions are: to accept or adopt reports, rati... ...on- firm action or to amend bylaws.

Since the main motion is the lowest ranking, all others except another main motion, take precedence over it and as before, may be made while it is pending. A main motion can only be made when there is no other matter of business before the assembly.

The main motion is always debatable. It requires a second and a majority vote except when: (1) by-laws require a greater vote, (2) adoption would be in conflict with something previously adopted, and (3) adoption would have the effect of suspending a rule of order to parliamentary right.

The motion should always be stated in the affirmative rather than the negative.

The proposer of a motion cannot debate against his motion but may vote against it. If a motion is long the chair may request the mover to put it in writing. If the motion is long, complex, or of special importance, it should be written in the form of a resolution.

RESOLUTION:

The usual wording of a resolution is, "I move the adoption of the following resolution: 'Resolved, That . . .'" or, "I offer the following resolution: 'Resolved, That . . .'"

It is usually inadvisable to attempt to include the reasons for a motion's adoption with the motion itself. Neither rule nor custom requires a resolution to have a preamble. However, special circum-

...ces make it desirable to include a brief statement or statements of background or reasoning. In this case a preamble should be used. It generally should contain no more clauses than are absolutely necessary.

If there is a preamble, each clause should be written as a separate paragraph, beginning with the word "Whereas" followed by a comma. The next word should begin with a capital letter. Regardless of how many paragraphs it has the preamble should never contain a period. Each of its paragraphs should close with a semicolon. In the next to the last paragraph the semicolon should be followed by the word "and." The last paragraph of the preamble should close with a semicolon, followed by a connecting expression such as "therefore" or "therefore, be it" or "now, therefore, be it." When one of these phrases is included, no punctuation should follow it, and it should always be placed at the end of the preamble paragraph, never at the beginning of the resolving paragraph, thus:

Whereas, The . . . (text of the preamble); now, therefore, be it

Resolved, That . . . (stating action to be taken).

The word "Resolved" is underlined or printed in italic. This is followed by a comma and the word "That" which begins with a capital "T."

There are times when more than one preamble clause and several resolving clauses are needed. In this case each should be a separate paragraph.

An example of how this is handled is listed below:

Whereas, The . . . (text of the first preamble clause);

Whereas, . . . (text of the next to the last preamble clause); and

Guide to Parliamentary Procedure

Whereas, . . . (text of the last preamble clause);

Resolved, That . . . (stating action to be taken);

Resolved, That . . . (stating further action to be taken); and

Resolved, That . . . (stating still further action to be taken.

Robert's Rules of Order Newly Revised, pages 27, 87-91

SUBSIDIARY MOTIONS

Subsidiary motions are assisting motions that help the assembly in the treatment and disposal of a motion. We deal with them here in the order of their priority and rank.

TO POSTPONE INDEFINITELY

Purpose:

The name of this motion is misleading. It actually does not mean to postpone. Its real purpose is to kill a motion or to allow the opposition the opportunity to see the assembly's attitude on the main question without having it actually come to a vote. Basic information:

MAY INTERRUPT?	A SECOND REQUIRED?	MAY BE DEBATED?	MAY BE AMENDED?	VOTE REQUIRED?	MAY BE RECONSIDERED?
NO	YES	YES	YES	MAJORITY	ONLY THE AFFIRMATIVE VOTE

TO AMEND

Purpose:

The purpose of a motion to amend is to change or improve the working of the pending motion in order to make it more acceptable.

MAY INTERRUPT?	A SECOND REQUIRED?	MAY BE DEBATED?	MAY BE AMENDED?	VOTE REQUIRED?	MAY BE RECONSIDERED?
NO	YES	YES	YES	MAJORITY	YES

Ways to Amend:
1. To insert or add words or provisions.
2. To strike out objectionable words or provisions.
3. To strike out and insert (strikes out objectionable words or provisions, and in its place inserts more acceptable words or provisions).
4. To substitute (whole paragraph or resolution).

An amendment must be germane, that is, it must have a definite relationship to the motion to which it is applied. An amendment may, however, be hostile to, or even defeat, the spirit or intent of the original motion and still be germane.

AMENDMENT TO THE MAIN MOTION (Amendment of the First Rank or Primary Amendment)

The purpose of this motion is to make the main motion more acceptable; therefore it must deal with the subject of the main motion. While it is possible to amend as many sections as desired, only one section can be amended at a time. While an amendment is pending it is proper to discuss only the amendment, not the main motion.

AMENDMENT TO THE AMENDMENT (Amendment of the Second Rank or Secondary Amendment).

The amendment to the amendment is basically handled under the same rules as the amendment to the main motion. The exception being, the amendment to the amendment cannot be amended. An amendment of the third degree would obviously make the parliamentary situation far too complicated.

Guide to Parliamentary Procedure

SUBSTITUTE MOTION

A substitute motion is used when it is desired to change an entire paragraph or resolution. The following rules apply. It must be properly proposed and seconded. It is a primary amendment and therefore, cannot be offered while there are other amendments on the floor.

The following procedural steps for handling a substitute motion have been suggested by R. Hollis Gause:

1. The substitute motion (being duly proposed and seconded) is temporarily set aside.

2. The assembly takes up the discussion of the original main motion. In this discussion the main motion may be amended as freely as if it were the only consideration of the house.

3. When this process is complete, the original main motion is temporarily set aside.

4. The assembly takes up the discussion of the substitute motion. In this discussion the substitute motion may be amended as freely as if it were the only consideration of the house.

5. The order of voting is as follows:

   a. The substitute motion is voted on first.

   b. If it passes, it becomes a main motion. The original main motion is lost. At this point the new main motion (formerly the substitute) is placed before the house for further debate and possible amendment.

   c. If the substitute fails to pass, the original main motion (as amended) remains the main motion. It is again subject to debate and possible amendment.

   d. A vote is taken on the motion (whether the substitute or the original main motion).

Administrative Resource Manual

TO REFER A COMMITTEE

Purpose:

The purpose of this motion is to delay action on the motion and put it in the hands of a small group of individuals who will gather further information, discuss it, and bring back their recommendations to the assembly.

Basic Information:

MAY INTERRUPT?	A SECOND REQUIRED?	MAY BE DEBATED?	MAY BE AMENDED?	VOTE REQUIRED?	MAY BE RECONSIDERED?
NO	YES	YES	YES	MAJORITY	YES*

*If the committee has not begun its work.

The motion should specify the kind (special or standing), size, power and manner of selection of the committee. It should include any special instructions as well as a time for the committee to report to the assembly. As soon as the committee has thoroughly researched and discussed the question referred to it, a well written, business-like, brief but clear report should be prepared. Usually one of the members (often the chairman) is chosen to prepare a draft of the report.

When the draft has been read to and approved by the committee, it should be signed by all the members who are in agreement with its contents. The report, usually given by the chairman, should contain the recommendation(s) of the committee along with any resolutions that might be necessary to effect the recommendation(s).

TO POSTPONE TO A CERTAIN TIME

Purpose:

The purpose of this motion is to delay consideration of the motion, usually for specific reasons, until a definite time.

Basic information:

Guide to Parliamentary Procedure

MAY INTERRUPT?	A SECOND REQUIRED?	MAY BE DEBATED?	MAY BE AMENDED?	VOTE REQUIRED?	MAY BE RECONSIDERED?
NO	YES	YES*	YES**	MAJORITY (2/3 SPECIAL ORDER)	YES

*Restricted to reasons for (propriety of), or time of, postponement.

**Restricted to time of postponement or as to Special or General Order.

The time of the postponement must be set, and must be no later than the next regular meeting. The motion to bring the matter back before the assembly is not necessary, since the motion to postpone at the last meeting is considered as unfinished business and automatically comes up for further consideration when unfinished business is in order.

TO LIMIT OR EXTEND LIMITS OR DEBATE

Purpose:

The purpose of this motion is to increase or decrease the allowable time of discussion on a particular issue. It may limit or extend in several ways: the number of speeches made, the number of minutes per speaker, or the total amount of time devoted to debate on the entire question.

Basic Information:

MAY INTERRUPT?	A SECOND REQUIRED?	MAY BE DEBATED?	MAY BE AMENDED?	VOTE REQUIRED?	MAY BE RECONSIDERED?
NO	YES	NO	YES	2/3	YES

Since this motion limits a basic parliamentary principle, that of full and free debate, two-thirds of the assembly must be in favor in order for the motion to pass. It applies only to the immediately pending question unless the motion specifies otherwise.

Administrative Resource Manual

TO CALL FOR THE PREVIOUS QUESTION

Purpose:

The name of this motion may be a bit puzzling to many, however, it simply means to stop debate and vote immediately on the pending question.

Basic information:

MAY INTERRUPT?	A SECOND REQUIRED?	MAY BE DEBATED?	MAY BE AMENDED?	VOTE REQUIRED?	MAY BE RECONSIDERED?
NO	YES	NO	NO	2/3	YES*

*But not after vote under it has been taken.

Since this motion limits a basic parliamentary principle, that of full and free debate, a two-thirds vote is required for passage. When members of the assembly call out informally, "Question!" it is usually their response to the chairman's query, "Are you ready for the question?" which simply indicates they are ready to vote on the pending question. It should be remembered that simply informally calling "Question, Question," is not moving the "Previous Question."

TO LAY ON THE TABLE

Purpose:

This motion is designed to allow the assembly to postpone temporarily the discussion and disposition of a pending issue in order to attend to more urgent business.

Basic information:

MAY INTERRUPT?	A SECOND REQUIRED?	MAY BE DEBATED?	MAY BE AMENDED?	VOTE REQUIRED?	MAY BE RECONSIDERED?
NO	YES	NO	NO	MAJORITY	NO

A motion cannot be taken from the table until another item of business has been transacted. After this transaction the motion may be taken from the table at any time. It must be dealt with before the end of the next meeting or it ceases to exist.

Guide to Parliamentary Procedure

PRIVILEGED MOTIONS

Privileged motions are motions of urgency, therefore, they have the right, or privilege, to interrupt debate on a pending motion and receive immediate attention. Actually, they may not necessarily have any bearing or direct relation to the business under discussion, but are related to the concerns of the assembly or of the individual members of the assembly.

The five privileged motions, listed in their order of rank are: to call for the orders of the day, to raise a question or privilege, to take a recess, to adjourn, and to fix the time to adjourn.

TO CALL FOR THE ORDERS OF THE DAY

Purpose:

The purpose of this motion is to enable the assembly to return to the specific order of established business after it has once deviated from that order.

Basic information:

MAY INTERRUPT?	A SECOND REQUIRED?	MAY BE DEBATED?	MAY BE AMENDED?	VOTE REQUIRED?	MAY BE RECONSIDERED?
YES	NO	NO	NO	NONE*	NO

*The chair decides.

If a member calls for the orders of the day, it is the responsibility of the chairman to bring the assembly back to the agenda unless objection is made. When a member objects, the chairman immediately puts the question to a vote. A two-thirds vote is required in the negative to refrain from returning to the predetermined order of business.

Administrative Resource Manual

TO RAISE A QUESTION OR PRIVILEGE

Purpose:

The purpose of this motion is to correct any undesirable condition and protect the rights of the assembly or of an individual member.

Basic information:

MAY INTERRUPT?	A SECOND REQUIRED?	MAY BE DEBATED?	MAY BE AMENDED?	VOTE REQUIRED?	MAY BE RECONSIDERED?
YES	NO	NO	NO	NONE*	NO

*The chair decides in most cases. However, if a question of privilege should result in having to take a vote the assembly decides, not just the chair. For example: A member rises and says he has a question of privilege. If it is that the room is too hot, or he cannot hear the speaker, the chair handles this. If his question of privilege is perhaps that people in the next room have important infomation on the question before the assembly, and he moves "that those people be invited into the meeting to give their views," someone has to second, and the pending question is set aside (not laid on the table, because after the question has been decided, the chair returns immediately to the question that had been under discussion, without having to wait for a motion to do so) while the question of privilege is considered. It is handled as any main motion.

This motion is often used to correct such things as: inability to hear the speaker, unnecessary noise, heating, cooling, ventilation, etc.

TO TAKE A RECESS

Purpose:

The purpose of this motion is to secure an intermission in the day's proceedings for a given time.

Basic information:

Guide to Parliamentary Procedure

MAY INTERRUPT?	A SECOND REQUIRED?	MAY BE DEBATED?	MAY BE AMENDED?	VOTE REQUIRED?	MAY BE RECONSIDERED?
NO	YES	NO	YES*	MAJORITY	NO

*Amendable as to the length of recess.

A motion to take a recess is a privileged motion only when another motion is pending, otherwise it is a main motion.

TO ADJOURN

Purpose:

The purpose of this motion is to terminate all business until the next regular meeting of the assembly.

Basic information:

MAY INTERRUPT?	A SECOND REQUIRED?	MAY BE DEBATED?	MAY BE AMENDED?	VOTE REQUIRED?	MAY BE RECONSIDERED?
NO	YES	NO	NO	MAJORITY	NO

Although a majority has voted in favor of the motion, the chair must declare the meeting adjourned before it is actually adjourned. After the vote has been taken, but before the chair has declared the meeting adjourned, any of the following may transpire:

1. The chairman may announce committees previously authorized.

2. A motion to reconsider may be made.

3. The motion to reconsider and enter in the minutes may be made.

4. Notices of any kind may be given.

5. Announcements, reminders of certain dates, etc., may be given.

The motion to adjourn may be in either the unqualified or qualified form. An example of an unqualified motion to adjourn would be: "I move that we adjourn." An example of a qualified motion to adjourn would be: "I move that we adjourn at 12:00

Administrative Resource Manual

o'clock noon." If the motion is introduced when no other motion is pending, it is a main motion rather than a privileged one.

The motion may not interrupt a speaker who has the floor. It would also be out of order while the assembly is engaged in voting or verifying a vote, or before the result of the vote has been announced by the chair. An exception would be in the case where the vote has been taken by ballot and the ballots have been collected by the tellers, but the results have not been announced.

TO FIX THE TIME TO ADJOURN

Purpose:

The purpose of this motion is to fix the time (and place) for an adjourned meeting to continue business as if there had been no interruption.

Basic information:

MAY INTERRUPT?	A SECOND REQUIRED?	MAY BE DEBATED?	MAY BE AMENDED?	VOTE REQUIRED?	MAY BE RECONSIDERED?
NO	YES	NO	YES*	MAJORITY	YES

*Amendable as to the date, hour or place.

It is a privileged motion only if it is introduced while another motion is pending, otherwise it is a main motion.

It should be remembered that if no time has been fixed for the next meeting, a motion to adjourn not only puts an end to the present meeting but also to any future meetings. Consequently, the motion to fix the time to adjourn is the highest motion possible. It is, therefore, in order even after a move to "Adjourn," if the chair has not declared the meeting adjourned.

Guide to Parliamentary Procedure

INCIDENTAL MOTIONS

This term describes a large body of motions of such nature that they arise only incidentally in the course of the business of the assembly. All incidental motions are not debatable except the motion to appeal from the decision of the chair, which has limited debate. Incidental motions have no rank among themselves. For this study we will limit our discussion to the following:

- To rise to a point of order
- To appeal from the decision of the chair
- To call for a division of the assembly
- To call for a division of the question
- To call for consideration by paragraph (or seriatim)
- To object to the consideration of a matter
- To make a parliamentary inquiry
- To withdraw or modify a motion
- To suspend the rules
- To make nominations
- To close nominations
- To reopen nominations

TO RISE TO A POINT OF ORDER

Purpose:

The purpose of this motion is to allow a member who feels that the business is not being conducted according to accepted parliamentary rules (usually Robert's Rules of Order Newly Revised) to object.

MAY INTERRUPT?	A SECOND REQUIRED?	MAY BE DEBATED?	MAY BE AMENDED?	VOTE REQUIRED?	MAY BE RECONSIDERED?
NO	NO	NO	NO	NONE*	NO

*The chair decides.

Administrative Resource Manual

TO APPEAL FROM THE DECISION OF THE CHAIR

Purpose:

The purpose of this motion is to allow a member who feels the chairman has made an error in his ruling the opportunity to appeal to the assembly for its opinion.

Basic information:

MAY INTERRUPT?	A SECOND REQUIRED?	MAY BE DEBATED?	MAY BE AMENDED?	VOTE REQUIRED?	MAY BE RECONSIDERED?
YES	YES	YES	NO	MAJORITY*	YES

*The decision of the chair will stand unless a majority votes to reverse it. A tie vote sustains the chair. The chairman (if a member of the assembly) may also cast the vote to make it a tie. In other words, it takes a majority vote in the negative to overturn the decision of the chair.

TO CALL FOR A DIVISION OF THE ASSEMBLY

Purpose:

The purpose of this motion is to determine the accuracy of a voiced vote.

Basic information:

MAY INTERRUPT?	A SECOND REQUIRED?	MAY BE DEBATED?	MAY BE AMENDED?	VOTE REQUIRED?	MAY BE RECONSIDERED?
YES	NO	NO	NO	NONE*	NO

*The chair decides.

Immediately after the chairman has announced the results of a voice vote, any member who doubts the chair's accuracy may call for a division of the assembly. When a call is made the chairman is obligated to take the vote again. This time the members are required to stand to indicate their vote. Another voice vote or the show of hands does not fulfill the requirement of a division of the assembly.

Guide to Parliamentary Procedure

TO CALL FOR A DIVISION OF THE QUESTION

Purpose:

The purpose of this motion is to allow for a more careful consideration of the question. It is used when a motion (either the main motion or an amendment) has two or more proposals, and there is a need or desire to discuss and act on the proposals individually.

Basic information:

MAY INTERRUPT?	A SECOND REQUIRED?	MAY BE DEBATED?	MAY BE AMENDED?	VOTE REQUIRED?	MAY BE RECONSIDERED?
NO	YES	NO	YES	MAJORITY	YES

When the motion is stated it should specify the manner in which the question is to be divided. After the division individual segments are treated as separate proposals.

TO CALL FOR CONSIDERATION BY PARAGRAPH (OR SERIATIM)

Purpose:

The purpose of this motion is to enable the assembly to deal with each individual paragraph (one at a time) of a long and detailed report.

Basic information:

MAY INTERRUPT?	A SECOND REQUIRED?	MAY BE DEBATED?	MAY BE AMENDED?	VOTE REQUIRED?	MAY BE RECONSIDERED?
NO	YES	NO	YES	MAJORITY	NO

This motion, which is often used in the adoption of bylaws, is usually handled by general consent. In following the provisions of this motion each paragraph is treated as if it were a main motion. When there is no further debate or amendments offered on the paragraph, the chairman calls up the next paragraph. This procedure is followed until all have been acted upon.

Administrative Resource Manual

However, no vote is taken on the individual paragraphs. It is only after all the paragraphs have been discussed that the entire body of material is presented to the assembly for debate, amendment and voting.

TO OBJECT TO THE CONSIDERATION OF A MATTER

Purpose:

The purpose of this motion is to avoid discussing contentions, irrelevant, unimportant or dilatory motions.

Basic information:

MAY INTERRUPT?	A SECOND REQUIRED?	MAY BE DEBATED?	MAY BE AMENDED?	VOTE REQUIRED?	MAY BE RECONSIDERED?
NO	NO	NO	NO	2/3	NO

This motion which only applies to the original main motion, must be made immediately after it is stated by the chairman, before any debate has occurred and before any subsidiary motion has been applied to it.

TO MAKE A PARLIAMENTARY INQUIRY

Purpose:

The purpose of this motion is to secure information which helps clear up confusing points of procedure, or to aid in the member's understanding of an issue.

Basic information:

MAY INTERRUPT?	A SECOND REQUIRED?	MAY BE DEBATED?	MAY BE AMENDED?	VOTE REQUIRED?	MAY BE RECONSIDERED?
YES	NO	NO	NO	NONE*	NO

*The chair decides.

TO WITHDRAW OR MODIFY A MOTION

Purpose:

The purpose of this motion is to allow a member who made a motion and later changed his mind

Guide to Parliamentary Procedure

the privilege of withdrawing or modifying the motion.

Basic information:

MAY INTERRUPT?	A SECOND REQUIRED?	MAY BE DEBATED?	MAY BE AMENDED?	VOTE REQUIRED?	MAY BE RECONSIDERED?
YES	NO	NO	NO	MAJORITY	AFF. NO*

*The chair decides.

It should be remembered that before a motion has been stated by the chair, its proposer has the right to withdraw it or modify it. However, after it has been stated, it can neither be withdrawn, nor modified without the consent of the assembly. After a motion has been stated by the chair it no longer belongs to the proposer, but rather, is the property of the assembly. A motion may, however, be withdrawn (by the mover) at any time before final action is reached, if there is no objection. If objection is voiced, a motion may be made by someone other than the mover to grant leave for withdrawing the motion.

Contrary to what is often heard or practiced in meetings, the second to a motion does not have to withdraw. If the mover modifies his motion the seconder may withdraw his second if he wishes.

TO SUSPEND THE RULES

Purpose:

The purpose of this motion is to temporarily suspend one or more of the rules contained in the parliamentary authority. The special rules of order, or the standing rules, that prohibit a course of action desired by at least two-thirds of the assembly.

Basic information:

MAY INTERRUPT?	A SECOND REQUIRED?	MAY BE DEBATED?	MAY BE AMENDED?	VOTE REQUIRED?	MAY BE RECONSIDERED?
NO	YES	NO	NO	2/3	NO

Administrative Resource Manual

It should be noted that certain rules cannot be suspended, such as: the fundamental principles of parliamentary procedure, rules that protect absent members, or rules that protect the rights of individual members of the assembly. Although it has not always been practiced, it is also impossible to suspend the Constitution and Bylaws unless a specific provision for their suspension has been made in the bylaws.

MOTIONS RELATING TO NOMINATIONS

TO MAKE NOMINATIONS
Basic information:

MAY INTERRUPT?	A SECOND REQUIRED?	MAY BE DEBATED?	MAY BE AMENDED?	VOTE REQUIRED?	MAY BE RECONSIDERED?
NO	NO	YES	NO	MAJORITY	YES

TO CLOSE NOMINATIONS
Basic information:

MAY INTERRUPT?	A SECOND REQUIRED?	MAY BE DEBATED?	MAY BE AMENDED?	VOTE REQUIRED?	MAY BE RECONSIDERED?
NO	YES	NO	YES	2/3	NO

The motion to close nominations is out of order if a member is seeking the floor in order to make a nomination.

TO REOPEN NOMINATIONS
Basic information:

MAY INTERRUPT?	A SECOND REQUIRED?	MAY BE DEBATED?	MAY BE AMENDED?	VOTE REQUIRED?	MAY BE RECONSIDERED?
NO	YES	NO	YES	MAJORITY	AFF. NO*

*Only

*Only a negative vote may be reconsidered.

Guide to Parliamentary Procedure

MOTIONS THAT BRING A QUESTION BEFORE THE ASSEMBLY AGAIN— RESTORATORY MOTIONS

Motions that bring a question before the assembly again enable the assembly, for good reason(s), to consider issues that have been previously disposed of. They may have been disposed of by being referred to a committee, postponed (indefinitely or to a certain time), laid on the table, passed or failed to pass.

TO TAKE FROM THE TABLE
Purpose:

The purpose of this motion is to resume consideration of a main motion that has been temporarily set aside (tabled).

Basic information:

MAY INTERRUPT?	A SECOND REQUIRED?	MAY BE DEBATED?	MAY BE AMENDED?	VOTE REQUIRED?	MAY BE RECONSIDERED?
NO	YES	NO	NO	MAJORITY	NO

When a motion is taken from the table it comes back to the assembly in the same form in which it was tabled. In other words, if any amendments or subsidiary motions were pending they must be dealt with in their order of precedence.

A motion cannot be taken from the table until another item of business has been transacted. After this transaction the motion may be taken from the table at any time. It must be dealt with before the end of the next meeting or it ceases to exist.

TO RESCIND (REPEAL OR ANNUL) OR AMEND SOMETHING PREVIOUSLY ADOPTED
Purpose:

The purpose of this motion is to render ineffective a vote previously taken. The motion to rescind

Administrative Resource Manual

may be used to strike out or annul an entire main motion, resolution, bylaw, section or paragraph that has been adopted. The motion to amend something previously adopted would be used to modify only a part of the wording or text previously adopted.

Basic information:

MAY INTERRUPT?	A SECOND REQUIRED?	MAY BE DEBATED?	MAY BE AMENDED?	VOTE REQUIRED?	MAY BE RECONSIDERED?
NO	YES	YES	YES	2/3*	YES**

*Majority vote with notice; two-thirds vote without notice; majority of entire membership without notice.

**Only a negative vote can be reconsidered.

A motion may be made to rescind and expunge from the minutes. Since nothing in the record can be obliterated, when the motion is expunged, the secretary simply draws a circle around that portion expunged, and writes expunged, the date, and his signature across the circle. That portion is excluded from any minutes published thereafter. Any action may be rescinded, except where the action taken cannot be undone, regardless of how old the action may be.

TO DISCHARGE A COMMITTEE

Purpose:

The purpose of this motion is to take the matter out of the hands of a committee. It allows the assembly itself to consider the issues, or it can be dropped.

Basic information:

MAY INTERRUPT?	A SECOND REQUIRED?	MAY BE DEBATED?	MAY BE AMENDED?	VOTE REQUIRED?	MAY BE RECONSIDERED?
NO	YES	YES	YES	2/3*	AFF. NO**

Guide to Parliamentary Procedure

*A majority vote with notice or a majority vote of the entire membership is required. Two special circumstances require only a majority vote:
1. If the committee failed to report as instructed within the prescribed time, and
2. While the assembly is considering any partial report of the committee.

**Only a negative vote can be reconsidered.

TO RECONSIDER A QUESTION
Purpose:

The purpose of this motion is to reopen for discussion and decision a matter previously considered and voted upon.

Basic information:

MAY INTERRUPT?	A SECOND REQUIRED?	MAY BE DEBATED?	MAY BE AMENDED?	VOTE REQUIRED?	MAY BE RECONSIDERED?
YES	YES	YES*	NO	MAJORITY	NO

*Undebatable only when the motion to be reconsidered is undebatable.

This motion, which is basically an American motion, makes a provision to correct a hasty or ill-advised action. The motion can be made only on the day that the vote to which it applies is made, or the next legislative day and it must be made by someone who voted with the prevailing side.

TO RECONSIDER AND HAVE ENTERED ON THE MINUTES
Purpose:

The purpose of this motion is to prevent a temporary majority from taking advantage of an unrepresentative attendance by voting on action that is opposed by a majority of the assembly. It simply means that the person making the motion gives notice to reconsider the motion at the next meeting. The motion must be made by someone who voted on the prevailing side, although anyone may second.

Basic information:

MAY INTERRUPT?	A SECOND REQUIRED?	MAY BE DEBATED?	MAY BE AMENDED?	VOTE REQUIRED?	MAY BE RECONSIDERED?
*	YES	NO	NO	**	NO

*See *Robert's Rules of Order Newly Revised* for exception or modification.
**NO vote is taken.

VOTING

The vote is the official decision or act of the assembly. Basic to each member is the right to vote and express his opinion. No member, however, can be compelled to vote. In fact, one should not vote on a question in which he has a direct personal or pecuniary interest not common to other members of the assembly. This rule does not prevent a member from voting for himself for an office or other position to which members are generally eligible.

BASIS FOR DETERMINING A VOTING RESULT

THE SIGNIFICANCE OF A MAJORITY VOTE

Basic to parliamentary procedure is the fundamental rule that requires at least a majority vote to take action. Majority means more than half the votes.

WHEN MORE THAN A MAJORITY VOTE IS REQUIRED

It has been mistakenly assumed by some that the higher the vote required, the greater the protection of the members. Actually, the opposite is true. When more than a majority is required, control is taken from the majority and given to the minority.

Guide to Parliamentary Procedure

WHEN LESS THAN A MAJORITY VOTE IS REQUIRED

When less than a majority vote is required, such as a plurality vote (more votes than any other candidate or alternative proposal) the same is true. The power of decision is taken from the majority and given to the minority.

THE MEANING OF THE MAJORITY VOTE

The term "majority" may have different meanings such as: a majority of all the membership, a majority of the members in a good standing, a majority of the members present, or a majority of a quorum. However, unless specified otherwise, a majority vote means a majority of the legal votes cast.

TWO-THIRDS VOTE

The term two-thirds vote, unless specified otherwise, means at least two-thirds of the legal votes cast. Any question which requires a two-thirds vote should be ascertained by taking a rising vote. A count should be taken if there is any doubt concerning the results.

PLURALITY VOTE

To receive a plurality vote simply means that more votes were received for this candidate or proposal than any other candidate or proposal.

UNANIMOUS VOTE

A unanimous vote is when a candidate or proposal received all the legal votes cast. In the case of a proposal the votes may be either in the affirmative or negative. When a vote is not unanimous, a motion to make it unanimous is out of order, unless that motion is also voted on by ballot.

METHODS OF VOTING

VOICE VOTE (VIVA VOCE)
By far the most common method of voting is by voice. The chair determines the result by the volume of voices. Both the vote for those in favor (Aye) and those opposed (No) must be taken. The affirmative vote should be taken first.

RISING OR RAISING HANDS
This method is used in verifying an inconclusive voice vote, or when a motion requires a two-thirds vote. In small assemblies a show of hands is used in place of a rising vote if no member objects. A show of hands is also used in place of a voice vote in small groups. When a rising vote is close or if there is any doubt as to the results of the vote, a count should be made.

ROLL CALL
When a record of each member's vote is desired a roll call vote is taken. This method is most often used when a member is a representative of others, for example, delegates, proxies, or members of governmental boards or commissions.

BALLOT
Voting by secret ballot is the only method whereby a member is able to express his decision without revealing his opinion or preference. Voting by secret ballot is usually required in elections and when voting on important proposals.

GENERAL (OR UNANIMOUS) CONSENT
In order to save time and expedite business, routine or non-controversial matters can be decided by general consent without taking a formal vote. If, however, a member objects a vote must be taken.

MAIL

Voting by mail can only be used if it authorized by the bylaws. This method, obviously, has many disadvantages and should only be used so long as it insures the members full understanding of the issues to be decided.

NOMINATIONS AND ELECTIONS

There are five methods of nominating: (1) by the chair, (2) from the floor, (3) by a committee, (4) by mail, and (5) by ballot. Perhaps the most commonly used methods in the church are by ballot and by a nominating committee. Our general and district bylaws usually specify that officers are to be elected by secret ballot. The first three ballots are usually nominating ballots and the next seven are designated as electoral ballots. However, if at any time any candidates received two-thirds of the votes an election is declared.

In meetings of any size tellers are usually appointed by the chair. The tellers are to see that the ballots are counted accurately, determine the legality of the ballots, and prepare a report of the results. The tellers' report should contain the following information: the total number of eligible votes, the number of votes cast, the number of votes needed for an election, and a list of the nominees, including the number of votes each received. The reporting teller (usually the chairman) reads the report without declaring the result. He then hands it to the chair who again reads it and declares the election if one has been reached. The ballots and tally sheets should be sealed in an envelope and given to the secretary who keeps them until it is certain a recount will not be ordered. They should then be destroyed.

MINUTES OF THE MEETING

The minutes are the official record of an organization. They should contain proceedings and actions taken by the assembly, not the discussion of the various members.

CONTENTS TO THE OPENING PARAGRAPH

The opening paragraph should contain the following information: (1) the kind of meeting (regular, special adjourned, annual, etc.), (2) the name of the organization, (3) the place where the meeting was called to order, (4) the date and time of the meeting, and (5) the name of the presiding officer.

ESSENTIAL ITEMS THAT SHOULD BE INCLUDED IN THE MINUTES

(1) The reading of the minutes of the last meeting. In most organizations, the first item of business, after establishing the presence of a quorum, is the reading of the minutes of the previous meeting. After the minutes have been read the chairman should ask, "Are there any corrections or additions? If none, the minutes will stand approved as read." If there are corrections the chairman will order the corrections to be made, and then state, "The minutes will stand approved as corrected." A formal motion to approve the minutes is not necessary. By a majority vote the correction of a mistake(s) may be made after the minutes have been approved (regardless of the amount of time that may have elapsed).

(2) All motions or resolutions, whether passed or lost, should be recorded in their exact wording along with the disposition of the motion. In the case of important motions, the name of the mover (but not the name of the seconder) should be given.

Guide to Parliamentary Procedure

(3) All points of order or appeals, whether sustained or lost, together with the reasons given by the chair for his rulings should be recorded in the minutes.

(4) The last paragraph should contain the time the meeting was adjourned.

(5) The minutes should be signed by the secretary. This authenticates them. Although the words "Respectfully Submitted" have for years preceded the signature, they are now considered outdated and no longer essential.

ADDITIONAL RULES AND PRACTICES RELATING TO THE CONTENT OF THE MINUTES

1) When a count has been ordered or a vote taken by ballot or roll call, the results should be recorded in the minutes.

(2) A summary of the reports of committees should also be recorded. When a report is of significant importance or of historical value, the entire report may be ordered to be included in the minutes.

(3) The minutes should be recorded in the third person, with the secretary being careful not to interject his personal opinion, interpretation or comments.

(4) A new paragraph should be used for each item of business. This makes it easier to read the minutes, as well as to research various items.

(5) It is best to record each new set of minutes on a new page.

GLOSSARY OF TERMS USED IN CONVENTIONS

Absentee Voting - Voting by mail or proxy (the member not being present), must be authorized by the bylaws.

Abstain - To refrain from voting.

Accept, Adopt, Approve - Applied to reports and motions agreed upon - not to be confused with "received".

Ad Hoc - A Latin term meaning "for this case alone" and used to designate a special or short-term committee.

Addressing the Chair - Using the appropriate title of the presiding officer when seeking recognition by the Chair.

Adjourn - To bring the meeting to a close.

Affirmative Vote - A vote of "Aye" or a vote in favor of the question.

Agenda - The order of business to be brought up at a meeting.

Alternate - A member authorized to take the place of another, if necessary as a delegate to a convention.

Amend - To change or modify a motion by striking out, by adding to, or by substituting.

Amendment - A motion which proposes to alter or modify a pending question.

Amendments to Bylaws - Motions which propose to change words, sections, or articles of the bylaws.

Annul - To rescind, repeal, or render voice.

Appeal from Chair's Decision - A request that the assembly sustain or reject the decision of the Chair.

Guide to Parliamentary Procedure

Appoint - To name or assign to an office or a committee.

Audit - Examination and verification of the society's financial record. (This report should be presented to the assembly for its adoption.)

Ballot Vote - A secret vote, usually on a slip of paper.

Blanks - Spaces left in a motion to be filled in by the assembly from a number of alternatives.

Budget - An estimate of probable income and expenditure for the ensuing year with proposals for maintaining a proper balance between the totals.

Business - Motion, resolution, subjects of the proceedings; the agenda.

Bylaws - Code of rules or regulations accepted by the constituency for its guidance.

Call for Orders of the Day - A motion used to call for a return to the scheduled order of business of the assembly.

Call to Order - A request by the presiding officer that the assembly come to order.

Carried - The motion has been adopted.

Caucus - A meeting to plan strategy toward a desired result within the assembly.

Chair - The presiding officer at a meeting.

Charter Members - The members of an organization who sign the bylaws when first adopted.

Commit - To refer to a committee.

Committee - One or more persons appointed to act on, consider, or report on, any matter.

Consideration of a Question - Deliberation by assembly after the chair has placed the motion before the assembly.

Constitution - Same as bylaws; sometimes combined, or in two parts. The constitution contains the more basic essentials; the other, procedures.

Convene - To meet together, or to be summoned to a meeting.

Convention - A meeting or formal assembly of delegates, normally chosen for one session only.

Credentials - A certificate proving one's right to the exercise of authority, or to claims or privileges. The Pentecostal Church of God grants three different credentials: Exhorter, Licensed, Ordained.

Debatable - That which is open to discussion.

Debate - To discuss the pros and cons of a motion.

Decision - A determination or ruling by the Chair.

Decorum (in Debate) - To behave with propriety; to conduct oneself in a proper manner.

Defer Action - To delay action on a motion by use of certain motions such as: to postpone, commit, or lay on the table.

Delegate - One sent to represent and act for others.

Dilatory Motion - An absurd or frivolous motion used to delay action.

Discharge (A Committee) - A motion to relieve a committee from further consideration of the task assigned to it.

Discussion - The debate that follows after the Chair has stated a debatable motion.

Disqualify - To declare ineligible.

Districts - Areas incorporated to do business in the name of the Pentecostal Church of God pertaining to these areas and as subsidiaries of the general church organization. Similar to states of the union.

Division of the Assembly - The motion that calls for a rising vote. The chair, if uncertain of the result, may take the vote again by a rising vote.

Guide to Parliamentary Procedure

Division of the Question - Separating a motion into two or more distinct parts for the purpose of debating and voting upon each part separately, as in a series of resolutions or amendments to by-laws.

Election - The selection of a person or persons by vote.

Entertain (A Motion) - As generally used, it is a request by the Chair for a formal motion on a subject which has been under discussion.

Ex Officio - By virtue of official position, usually of boards or committees.

Executive Committee - Committee of administrators and department heads who process and conduct business in the interim between General Board meetings.

Executive Session - A meeting at which the proceedings are secret.

Expunge - The act of drawing a line through the offending words in the minutes.

Extended Debate - A motion to prolong debate.

Fee Simple - An estate of land inheritable by the heirs generally of the holder of the estate without restriction to any particular class of heirs.

Fiscal Year - The financial year of an organization.

Fix the Time to Adjourn - A motion to adjourn the meeting at a specified time.

Floor, Obtain the - When a member is recognized by the Chair, he has the "floor."

General Consent - Unanimous, silent, used in routine matters, if there is no objection, avoiding a formal vote.

Germane - Closely related to an having a direct bearing upon; used in relation to amendments which must be germane to the motion being amended.

Hostile - Unfriendly or opposed.

In Order - Correct procedure from a parliamentary standpoint.

Incidental Motion - A motion that arises out of a question that is or has just been pending and must be disposed of before the pending question or other business is acted on.

Indefinite Postponement - A subsidiary motion to defer consideration of a main motion for an indefinite time, proposed for the purpose of killing the main motion.

Information (Request For) - An incidental motion seeking information relating to pending business.

Inquiry (Parliamentary) - An incidental motion seeking information relating to pending business.

Lay on the Table - The highest ranking subsidiary motion which enables the assembly to lay the pending question aside temporarily when something more urgent has arisen.

Limit Debate - A subsidiary motion used to reduce the time for debate on a motion.

Lost Motion - A motion on which the majority, or in some cases two-thirds, of the votes cast are "no."

Main Motion - The motion that introduces the business or a proposal to the assembly for action.

Majority - More than half the votes cast.

Marriage Questionnaire - A list of questions to be completed regarding a former marriage of a credential applicant or companion.

Minutes - The official record of proceedings at a meeting.

Guide to Parliamentary Procedure

Motion - A proposal that something be done or opinion expressed upon a subject.

MSC - Motion, seconded and carried.

Negative Vote - A vote against the adoption of the question being considered.

New Business - New matters presented to the assembly for consideration.

Nomination - The formality of naming a person as a candidate for appointment or election.

Null and Void - Having no legal effect.

Object to Consideration - A motion to avoid the discussion on some undesirable or delicate subject. This can only be applied to an original main motion.

Obtaining the Floor - Securing recognition in order to speak; means that a member has risen, addressed the Chair by his correct title, and the Chair has responded by nodding or announcing his name.

Opposed - Against the adoption of the question under consideration.

Order of Business - The agenda; the schedule of business to be considered.

Ordered - Directed by vote of the assembly.

Orders of the Day - The program or business of the meeting arranged as prescribed by the rules or vote of the assembly.

Out of Order - A motion or request which cannot be entertained at that time.

Parliamentarian - One who is knowledgeable about parliamentary procedure; one who advises the presiding officer concerning matters of parliamentary procedure.

Parliamentary Inquiry - An incidental motion raising a question about parliamentary procedure.

Administrative Resource Manual

Pending - A motion is said to be pending after it has been stated by the Chair and is under consideration.

Pending Question - The question or questions that are under consideration.

Pentecostal Messenger - The official publication of the Pentecostal Church of God.

Personal Privilege - A question raised by a member which concerns the health, safety, and integrity of the member or of the assembly.

Plurality - Term used in an election when one candidate has the largest number of votes.

Plurality Vote - The largest number of votes received when there are three or more choices.

Point of Order - A question concerning a breach of parliamentary rules.

Postpone - To defer action on a question indefinitely or until a certain time.

Postpone Indefinitely - A motion to suppress, eliminate, or "kill" the main motion.

Precedence - Rank. (Certain motions have priority over other motions.)

Precedent - A decision or course of action, serving as a rule for future determination in similar cases.

Prevailing Side - The winning side; the side having procured the greatest number of votes.

Previous Question - A call to close debate and take the vote.

Privileged Motion - A motion, not related to pending business, of such importance that it has the right to interrupt the pending question.

Pro Tem (Pro Tempore) - Temporarily; usually applied to one who serves in the absence of the regular officer or chairman, as "Secretary protem," or "Chairman pro tem."

Guide to Parliamentary Procedure

Proxy (Vote) - A vote authorized by, and cast on behalf of, a member who is absent.

Putting the Question - Placing the motion before the assembly.

PYPA - Pentecostal Young People's Association.

PYPA Central Committee - A committee made up of the presidents and general officers of the Pentecostal Young People's Association.

Question - Same as motion, when stated by the Chair for a vote.

Question of Privilege - A privileged motion asking permission to make an urgent request affecting the rights of an individual or the assembly.

Quorum - A specified number of members required, according to the bylaws, to hold a legal meeting.

Ratify - An incidental main motion to approve action already taken, but which requires a vote of the assembly to make the action valid.

Recess - A short intermission within a meeting, approved by the members.

Recognizing a Member - Acknowledging by the Chair, a member who has the right to address the assembly.

Recommendation - The expression of opinion or advice, usually from a committee, on a motion referred to it for study.

Recommit (Same as Commit) - To refer again to committee for further consideration.

Reconsider - A motion to take up for consideration a second time the vote on a previously adopted or defeated question. If adopted, the question is again before the assembly in its original state, for discussion and decision by the assembly.

Reconsider and Enter on the Minutes - A motion to stop action on a question and to give the assembly an opportunity to reconsider the question when a more representative attendance can be obtained.

Recount - To recount the vote again.

Refer - To submit a subject or a motion to a committee for consideration.

Renew (A Motion) - To place on the floor, at a succeeding session, a motion previously defeated.

Rescind - To annul action previously adopted.

Resignation - A formal notice stating that one is relinquishing his office or position.

Resolution - A formal proposal offered to, or a formal expression of opinion by, a legislative assembly or public meeting.

Roll Call - Calling the names of all members to determine the presence of a quorum.

Roll Call Vote - A vote taken by calling the names of all members, for the purpose of recording how each member votes. The president's name is called last.

Rules of Order - Written rules by which the organization is governed.

Ruling - A decision made by the presiding officer.

Second - An indication by a second person of a willingness to have the motion discussed (generally made by one who is in favor of the motion).

Session - A meeting of an organization or a series of connected meetings as in a convention.

Speaker - One who has obtained the floor and has begun to address the assembly.

Special Committee - A committee chosen to perform some special function after which it automatically ceases to exist.

Special Meeting - A meeting called for a specific purpose which must be stated in the call.

Guide to Parliamentary Procedure

Standing Committees - Permanent committees that perform continuing functions for the life of the assembly that established them. (Usually listed in the bylaws.)

Standing Rules - Rules of temporary or semi-permanent nature relating to details of administration rather than Parliamentary Procedure.

Stating the Question - Restatement, by the Chair, of a motion made by a member in order to place the motion before the assembly for debate.

Sub-Committee - A committee selected by the parent committee for the purpose of studying and investigating certain matters; responsible tax report to the Committee not to the Assembly.

Substitute (Amendment) - An amendment which proposes to strike out a paragraph, section, or resolution and insert another in its place.

Suspend (the Rules) - A motion to make ineffective for a limited time a rule of an organization.

Sustain - To support and uphold a ruling.

Table a Motion - To put aside the pending question temporarily.

Take From the Table - A motion used to return a question to the assembly which had been tabled.

Tellers - Individuals officially designated to count ballots or votes.

Tie Vote - Same number of votes on either side; a lost vote on a motion (except appeal) no election.

Two-thirds Vote - Two-thirds of the votes cast by persons legally entitled to vote.

Unanimous Vote - Unanimous consent; no dissenting vote; general consent.

Undebatable Motion - A motion on which debate is not permitted.

Unfinished Business - Matters on the agenda of a previous meeting on which no action was taken.

Administrative Resource Manual

Vacancy - An unoccupied office or position.

Viva Voce Vote - A voice vote.

Vote - A formal expression of opinion or choice, either positive or negative, made by a member or a group of members.

Vote by Acclamation - The spontaneous approval of a candidate by unanimous viva voce vote.

Withdraw a Motion - To remove a motion from consideration by the assembly upon request by the mover, and by permission of the assembly if motion has been stated by the Chair.

Yield - Concede to, outranked by, give way to.

Yielding the Floor - The speaker gives of his time in order that another may speak or address the assembly.

- SECTION FIVE -

MISCELLANEOUS INFORMATION

The design of this manual is to be concise. We have combined various subject material under the section of Miscellaneous Information.

Along with the chapter titles mentioned below, the titles offered in the chapter on Bibliography provide a vast resource on various subjects.

As it has been noted previously this manual is intended to provide a resource for administration and as such it would be impossible to provide a one volume exhaustive study on such an important subject.

The chapters in Section Five are:
- Chapter 21 — Notes on District Accounting and Audit Procedures
- Chapter 22 — Congregationalism and the Pentecostal Church of God
- Chapter 23 — Financial Support/Structure
- Chapter 24 — Annual Church Report
- Chapter 25 — Job (Position) Descriptions
- Chapter 26 — Communication
- Chapter 27 — Bits and Pieces
- Chapter 28 — Bibliography

Administrative Resource Manual

CHAPTER 21

District Accounting

PURPOSES FOR ACCOUNTING AS RELATED TO DISTRICTS

Accounting is the process whereby the financial transactions for a period are recorded and summarized in logical and meaningful fashion so as to reaveal clearly and succinctly the experience and financial condition of the district. District officers serve as custodian of district funds and are responsible for the adequacy of the accounting process.

Good accounting is not complex. Facts are never hidden under a lot of complex reports. The best reports are succinct, clear and organized according to generally accepted accounting models. Good accounting accomplishes the following:
• It produces reports which accurately reflect the experience and condition of the entity.
• It reveals trends for effective administration of the financial affairs of the district.
• It enables better decisions by furnishing clear, meaningful and accurate information.

Notes on District Accounting and Audit Procedures

TYPES OF ACCOUNTING

Although manual bookkeeping is almost extinct, it survives in some very small entities. The use of computers generally replaced manual accounting. The lower cost of computers and the many functions they can furnish even a small district make them a viable choice for about every situation.

MANUAL ACCOUNTING

At the minimum, an adequate minimum set of books for a district would include a combined cash journal and a general ledger. To this might be added other journals to track such things as Home Missions notes receivable, pledges etc. Manual accounting is limited to a very few accounts because of space limitations, and generally results in more complex and less meaningful reports. These are also much more difficult to audit properly and are subject to accounting errors.

COMPUTERIZED ACCOUNTING

The computer and the newer software now available has simplified the accounting process and in many instances, reduced costs for districts. Most districts keep their books in what is termed fund accounting, a process whereby established funds carry running balances and appear in reports as independent accounting. This furnishes better control of such funds as Home Missions etc. The Pentecostal Church of God has adopted the Parsons Money Counts software as a standard for accounting because it is the only inexpensive software which supports fund accounting. While it does not do individual receipting, there are solutions for those who wish to move beyond the older District Re-

Administrative Resource Manual

ceipt Program. The General Office can furnish advice and help in this area.

REPORTS

The use of standardized reports solves a variety of problems. These are usually easier to understand and are familiar to many people inasmuch as they are used by both the business and the church world. These include at minimum: (1) Statement of Operations, and (2) Balance Sheet. Districts operated essentially on a cash basis but for a Balance Sheet to reflect changes in position accurately, should make certain adjustments at the end of a report period to accomplish this. These are:

1. Recognition of prepaid expenses (insurance, postage, etc.).
2. Adjustment for changes in amount owed on Accounts Payable.
3. Adjustment for any capital account changes which did not go through the checking account. This can include such things as changes in notes receivable, donated items, tracking of estimated net church worth for all churches if used, etc.

Some districts follow the practice of showing estimated net worth for local church properties. These are accumulated through annual reports from the churches, and might be used, but in all events, should be shown as estimated value, or accompanied by a note explaining the basis for the computation. When a district's balance sheet is used as security for loans, care must be taken that all assets shown be accurate and clearly defined.

DEPRECIATION: Inasmuch as churches and church organizations need not use depreciation for costing capital acquisitions, it is difficult for some to understand why district assets should be depreciated. One reason is that it makes the balance sheet standard and lending institutions are accustomed to seeing this and making allowances for the difference between book value and real value. Failure to use depreciation often raises questions regarding how trustworthy the accounting is for genuine appraisal of financial condition. It is good practice to make annual depreciation adjustments for all assets except land.

ACQUISITIONS: Another practice which is frowned on by financial institutions is that of placing an acquisition on the books at an estimated worth rather than the true monetary cost. This is considered improper although current procedures do make allowance for donated labor and materials providing an accurate and fair record is kept in detail to support the value placed on the asset. Inflating an asset at the point of acquisition can make us feel good but can come back to haunt us when we dispose of the asset and must make the downward adjustment on the next balance sheet.

ACCOUNTING PROCEDURES

Good accounting not only requires careful and proper recording of all transactions but also timely and prompt handling of these. Books should be completed and balanced at the end of every month and reports placed on file. Detailed listing of all transactions should be part of the monthly file.

INTERNAL CONTROLS: It is important that internal controls be in place for the protection of those who are custodians of funds and administration. All offerings taken in public meetings should be counted by no less than two persons other than those with check-signing privileges. A written summary of the offering should be made and kept in file. The use of cash is discouraged, and if used, should be supported by a detailed file showing receipts or details of all funds so handled. It is better procedure to make all payments by check. Reimbursements should be recorded so as to reflect the accounting detail of the transaction. Where a reimbursement covers more than one type of expense, the transaction should be split to show exactly what expense was charged. Receipts or other documentation should be kept in file to support any reimbursement payment.

RECEIPTING: While it is the practice of some districts to send no receipts until the end of the year, this provides little protection for improper data entry. The sending of receipts accomplishes two worthy purposes: (1) It provides an opportunity for the district office to communicate with the donor, and (2) it provides a method for certifying that the funds were credited to the proper area of accounting. There should be a clear correlation between the receipts and deposits made to the bank.

DISTRICT AUDIT PROCEDURES

Districts follow a variety of methods for annual audits of the district accounting. Some use independent auditors and others make use of an auditing committee. Whatever the process, the following is suggested as a framework for such audits.

The purpose of a financial audit is twofold: (1) To assess and render an opinion as to the accuracy and completeness of the accounting process used, and (2) to prepare and/or review the reports to be furnished to the board and convention.

Notes on District Accounting and Audit Procedures

There are some things which are important in performing an audit:

1. Are the beginning balances for the accounting reports the same as reported in the previous reports and audit?
2. Does a complete computation of all transactions begin with the ending balances from the prior year produce the ending results shown in the reports?
3. Do deposited funds in banks or institutions reflect the same as those shown on the reports?
4. Does a random sampling of receipts and deposits indicate that care is given to properly account for all received funds?
5. Are there any contingent liabilities not reflected in the reports (such as signing as security for loans etc.)?
6. Are all changes of net worth reflected accurately and fairly?
7. Does the district follow generally accepted rules and forms for accounting and reporting? If not, are the exceptions defensible?
8. Are there credible documentation supporting any use of cash funds or reimbursements?
9. Are all payments to persons in accordance with district bylaws or board decisions?
10. Are there bank statements and other documentation supporting funds reflected in the reports?
11. Are all adjustments made to the accounting process supported by proper documentation?

CHAPTER 22
Congregationalism and The Pentecostal Church of God

It is easy to form assumptions as to the meaning of a word. However, words cannot be properly defined in isolation from history and accepted usage. A statement in the *General Constitution and Bylaws* of the Pentecostal Church of God has been the subject of considerable misuse and misapplication. That statement is:

"The Pentecostal Church of God now has, and shall always maintain, a representative and congregational form of government" (Article Four, page 27).

Historical Meaning: Congregationalism, as practiced in America, grew out of the Church of England, coming to America with the Pilgrims. This designation was based on the autonomy of each congregation. These Congregationalists were opposed to Presbyterianism which included organization by means of district and national bodies. Typically, Congregationalism "acknowledges no earthly authority beyond the local" *(Grollier's Encyclope-*

Congregationalism and the Pentecostal Church of God

dia). The following is from the Hammer text on Church and Law:

> What is a "hierarchical church"? One legal authority defines "hierarchical" and "congregational" churches as follows:
>
> At least three kinds of internal structure, or "polity," may be discerned: congregational, presbyterial, and episcopal. In the congregational form each local congregation is self-governing. The presbyterial polities are representative, authority being exercised by laymen and ministers organized in an ascending succession of judicatories—presbytery over the session of the local church, synod over the presbytery, and general assembly over all. In the episcopal form power reposes in clerical superiors, such as bishops. Roughly, presbyterial and episcopal polities may be considered hierarchical, as opposed to congregational polities, in which the autonomy of the local congregation is the central principle. 49 Note, Judicial Intervention in Disputes Over the Use of Church Property, 75 Harvard Law Review 1142, 1143-44 (1962).

A truly congregational form of government involves the following:

1. The local church recognizes no authority over them except God.

2. Church membership requirements are determined by the local church.

3. All property is held solely in the name of the local body.

4. All ministers are ordained by the local church.

5. Local churches and pastors are accountable only to the local membership.

6. All discipline for any cause is solely at the discretion of the local church.

7. No associative assembly is used inasmuch as all authority is local.

Administrative Resource Manual

8. The church board, as elected representatives, hold authority over the pastor.

Pentecostal Church of God Polity: It is inaccurate to single one statement out of a document and infer that such statement alone defines the polity of the entity. Here are some internal evidences to show that we are not and have not for many years been a truly congregational organization. Following the above outline of congregationalism, here is how the Pentecostal Church of God differs. The designations (9:1:a, 27) will briefly reference the 1998 edition of the Bylaws as: (Article:Section:paragraph, page) for brevity.

1. The local church recognizes no authority over them except God.

The General Bylaws clearly show that the highest authority in the Pentecostal Church of God is the General Convention. Authority is specifically forbidden to any leader, national or district (7:9, 31). While churches may elect their own pastors, restrictions are imposed (13:9, 10, 38).

2. Church membership requirements are determined by the local church.

The General Bylaws establish some national requirements for membership in local churches (13:9, 38).

3. All property is held solely in the name of the local body.

The General Bylaws clearly provide restrictions on titles for church property in the name of the organization (13:1:a-c, 36). They also provide that property be vested in the district and that any church holding property in its own name must have a reversionary clause in the

Congregationalism and the Pentecostal Church of God

deed (13:5, 37).
4. All ministers are ordained by the local church.
All credentials are granted at the national level after approval by the district. All ministers are amenable to their district. (Article 14 in its entirety, and 15:1, 43).
5. Local churches and pastors are accountable only to the local membership.
Both pastors and churches are accountable to the movement through their respective district (15:1, 43 and 13:5, 37).
6. All discipline for any cause is solely at the discretion of the local church.
Discipline of ministers is assigned to the district with appeal privileges to the General Board (Article 15, pages 43-46).
7. No associative assembly is used inasmuch as all authority is local.
Ministers and churches comprise the constituency recognized by biennial General Conventions (Article 7, pages 30, 31).
8. The church board, as elected representatives, hold authority over the pastor.
While the General Bylaws do not clearly define the relationship between a pastor and the local church board, the recommended Bylaws used by many of our churches as a model and published by the General Office provide that the pastor is the "spiritual overseer of the church" and the board acts "in an advisory capacity with the pastor in all matters pertaining to the church in its spiritual life . . . ."

From the above it is clear that the Pentecostal Church of God is **not** congregational in polity. The same clause which defines the movement as "congregational" also defines it as "representative," or democratic. In reality, there are only three forms of government practiced in churches and the Pentecostal revival has a fair representation of all three. These are:

Episcopal: This form of polity is patterned after the Catholic and Anglican churches, and places all power under the "bishops" of whatever title. This has been described as "The bishop hears from God and the people hear from the bishop." American Pentecostal bodies which practice some degree of this form of polity include the Church of God (Cleveland) and the Pentecostal Holiness Church.

Modified Presbyterian: This form of church government organizes churches into districts and the districts combine to form a national and international church. Included in this form of polity are the Pentecostal Church of God, Assemblies of God, Open Bible Standard, International Church of the Foursquare Gospel and other similar bodies. On the whole, these have been some of the most prolific in growth over the past century.

Congregational: This form of government in its true meaning is practiced only by the independent Pentecostals. The moment a group of ministers or churches unite for more effective ministry and oversight they are no longer truly congregational.

While we have a strong emotional attachment to the idea of congregationalism, the fact is that most truly congregational bodies have been the result of a split or begun by dissidents who are not willing to work under authority or oversight.

The word **hierarchical** has been used to define denominations, and again a look at the history of

Congregationalism and the Pentecostal Church of God

Christianity gives us perspective on the true meaning of the term.

> Webster describes hierarchy as: "a system of church government by priests or other clergy in graded ranks: 2. the group of officials, esp. the highest officials, in such a system. 3. a group of persons or things arranged in order of rank, grade, class, etc."

If leadership comes from the top down in any form, it is hierarchical. This does not imply that it is Episcopal, however. Any levels of leadership constitute hierarchical levels and may be properly defined as hierarchical in form. The structure Jesus used in forming the Early Church was truly hierarchical. The Early Church expanded that very quickly when it became evident that without authority and oversight the door was opened for all kinds of attacks from the enemy. Historically in America most of the churches which began as congregational soon moved to some form of organization which automatically established some form of hierarchical structure. To confuse the term hierarchical with episcopal is to overlook much of the history of the Christian Church.

CHAPTER 23
Financial Support/Structure

Through the years the financial structure has evolved to its present status. We have a promoted and legislated fiscal structure as opposed to a unified budget program.

The local church supports its pastor and church by the tithes and offerings of the people. The pastor is supported either by receiving the tithe, or a percentage of the tithe or a salary from the general fund of the church. Generally, the larger churches support their pastor by salary.

The district office and officers are supported by the tithes of the ministers in the district, the offerings from churches and sectional fellowship. The officers are paid a percentage of the tithe or a salary.

The General Office and officers are supported by the tithes from the members of the General Board, the credential fees of ministers, the 5% participation plan and sales of printed materials.

The departments of ministry are supported by offerings and gifts by the constituency through individual promotion.

Financial Support/Structure

The General Offices exist to coordinate the church's ministry world-wide, to promote the purpose of existence and serve the constituency so that we may function on all levels of operation.

It is evident that a type of unified budget is needed which could provide better stewardship and effectiveness of mission and purpose.

THE 5% BUDGET SUPPORT PLAN
The 5% Support Base for General Headquarters

The General Convention in June 1975 adopted a support program calling for 5% of the operational budget of each local church with an annual participation maximum set at $600.00 per church. The program was adopted on a two-year trial period.

The General Convention in June 1977 reviewed the support program, and after an amendment was added, it was subsequently adopted as a regular and permanent support program for General Headquarters. The promotional efforts, designed to create a proper understanding of the 5% program, has experienced some success. However, to develop a broader knowledge to insure total participation in the program, this information is provided. This equitable percentage support program has the potential of meeting the monthly operational need of our ongoing ministries, with the full cooperation of all our churches. Obviously, no program can experience full success without full cooperation.

The 5% Participation Support Plan Adopted by the General Convention Body

After many hours of research and exchange of ideas for plans of a support base for General Headquarters, and after the experience acquired by a

Administrative Resource Manual

two-year trial period of the 5% plan, the following resolution was adopted by the 1977 General Convention making the 5% a regular and permanent support program.

THE RESOLUTION:

"Whereas there is need for establishing an adequate financial base under the ministries of the Pentecostal Church of God, therefore, be it resolved that all our churches shall support the General Headquarters at a rate of five percent of the operational budget of each local church, with a maximum annual participation required set at $600 per church. Churches not complying will lose their church delegate per 100 members as presently recorded in the assessment area of the bylaws. Each district shall contribute five percent of their operational funds. The pastor of each member congregation shall be charged with the responsibility of providing the leadership necessary to insure the participation of his congregation in the financial program. Said five percent support program shall be a regular and permanent support program. The promotional responsibility to insure 100% participation shall be delegated to three levels of leadership: The General Superintendent, all District Superintendents, and all Pastors."

The percentage plan of support is an equitable program for all churches. It is a remarkable plan, and deserving of 100% cooperation and participation. The five percent plan replaces the old $12 per year per church assessment. It assures our future operation, as we grow together with full participation, the needed increase will be provided.

Financial Support/Structure

SUPPORT PLAN

The 5% Plan Explained

5% to Headquarters (Operational Budget)
- Church maintenance
- Sunday school
- Mortgage payments
- Utility payments
- Advertising
- Tax required payments
- Salary for staff personnel
- Miscellaneous expenses

Excluded from 5% (Promotional Funds)
- Pastor's salary
- Evangelism offerings
- Foreign Missions
- Indian Missions
- Home Missions
- PYPA projects
- Women's Ministries projects
- Messenger College
- Offerings for new construction

In other words, five percent is to be paid on all the cost incurred in operating the church locally. Just exclude pastor's salary and promotional offerings.

An Example of Monthly Expenses:

Pastor's salary	$1,000.00
Staff salaries	500.00
Church building payments	400.00
Sunday school	200.00
World Missions	350.00
Indian Missions	150.00
Revival	350.00
Messenger College	100.00

Administrative Resource Manual

PYPA	100.00
Gross Budget	$3,150.00
Less:	
Pastor's salary	1,000.00
World Missions	350.00
Indian Missions	150.00
Revival	350.00
PYPA	100.00
Messenger College	100.00
Net Operating Budget	$1,100.00
5% Participation for Headquarters:	
per month	$55.00

(Maximum of $600 per year required.)

Simply, each member church pays 5% of the monthly budget or cost for operating the local church. If it costs $1,500 a month for operation, after excluding pastor's salary and promotional offerings for ministries, you pay $75 less $25, making a total of $50 which is the maximum required amount montly.

This program presently produces over $150,000 per year with an average of about 61% of churches participating faithfully each month. Its potential could be about $250,000 with 100% participation.

The General Constitution and Bylaws provide that the General Superintendent, General Secretary and General Business Manager are to present a General Office budget each November to the General Board and the portion not covered by anticipated receipts is to be proportionally divided among the districts to raise in any manner they wish.

Financial Support/Structure

We have suggested that each district leader and pastor use the 5% as a means to bring the district part of the annual general budget.

It is working. It has great potential, but needs full cooperation of leadership to promote, explain and encourage all to participate.

Administrative Resource Manual

Chapter 24
Annual Church Report

Statistics can seem to be a dull subject. In fact, statistics are at the heart of America's (and the world's) most advanced growth in the fields of business, finance and corporate planning. Without good statistics it is not possible to make meaningful long range plans.

For statistics to have meaning it is important that some fundamental principles be observed. In the church field, different denominations choose a variety of areas for study and sometimes use differing yardsticks for measuring. What is important is that the rule used in measuring be consistent, and for any comparison between ourselves and others, that we use similar modes of reporting.

Annual Local Church Report. The ALCR is intended as a tool for the leaders of the local church by which they evaluate their ministry. Is growth taking place? If so, where? Why? or vice-versa. Is Jesus pleased with what we are doing? The primary ministry of our movement is taking place in the local church.

Annual Church Report

When all the ALCRs are received and totals computed it helps us to realize who we are and what we have accomplished together. These combined or averaged figures are the ones used for reporting and comparison.

Prior to 1997 we took the average of the responses on the ALCR and multiplied that number by our number of churches to get the totals we reported. We have discovered this is not an acceptable approach in professional circles. It is our understanding that we should only report what is actually reported to us. Therefore you can easily understand why it is important that we receive a report from every church.

Outreach. The questions dealing with the number saved, filled with the Holy Ghost and baptized in water help to determine the spiritual impact the ministries of our church is experiencing. In many cases educated approximations will be necessary to answer these questions.

Sunday School Attendance. If your entire Sunday school program involves a single time on Sunday, this is an easy number to reach. However, churches today often have special educational outreaches such as neighborhood Sunday (or Saturday) school programs, Sidewalk Sunday schools (which may take place on another day) or teaching ministries in nursing homes etc. It is generally accepted that such outreach ministries may be combined with the church-based Sunday school program to arrive at a total.

Average Sunday Morning Attendance. This is the number you have present for the Sunday morning worship service. Some churches have more than one Sunday morning service, in which case it would be the total of the attendance from all services. Inasmuch as this attendance may not be one where an official count is taken, some educated approximations may be necessary and appropriate.

Church Membership. Some denominations have a practice of retaining virtually all members unless a request is received for transfer to another congregation. For these bodies, membership is their single largest statistical number. You should count all active and inactive members who are listed on your church records.

Constituency. Some use "adherents" for this same purpose and we may assume that the meaning is essentially identical. What this means is the total number of people of all ages who consider your church their home church. This includes people who only come occasionally, those who are too ill or feeble to attend and others who would call on your church or pastor for family counseling, weddings, funerals etc. This number is usually about twice the average attendance. It is an estimate, but should be a measure of the total impact of your church on your community.

Financial and Property Information. We do request some financial information similar to that collected by a number of our districts. Be assured that this is never used or released in any single-church report, nor is it ever identified with any particular church. The numbers you furnish are combined with others to furnish averages and other statistical information. Financial information is appreciated but not required.

Our Appreciation. We deeply appreciate your effort to help us obtain the most accurate and complete information possible so that we might track our total ministry in a meaningful way. Not every church is experiencing rapid growth but many of our Pentecostal Churches of God are. Not all our churches are improving their facilities or building new ones but we do have many who have and are. The only way we can track the total picture of what is going on in the statistical field is with such surveys.

We recognize that numbers are not the best evidence of what God is doing in your church. You can't count blessings, lives changed, miracles and the spiritual growth of our people, and we recognize that that is the most vital of all that happens. Numbers and dollars do not measure the total of what God is doing, but it is one way to indicate what is happening because of the spiritual outpouring.

CHAPTER 25
Job (Position) Descriptions

A job description, sometimes called position description depending on the job, is very important as it helps us know our task and why we are in the organization. A job description helps our superior to know what we are doing. It helps us to know what he expects of us, and lets people around us know what we are doing. Likewise, we know why their jobs exist.

Job descriptions are similar yet can be tailored uniquely to various positions. However, in any case, it is imperative to communicate the provisions contained therein clearly to the individual.

Inasmuch as the bylaws, policy manual or other guides represent only a brief job duty, it is necessary to detail a job description for each position for efficient and effective work performance.

Job Description Definition

"A job description is an organized summary of the duties and responsibilities involved in a position."

Job (Position) Descriptions

The summary of duties and responsibilities in any position is to be used as a guide, not an inflexible standard which inhibits the spiritual gifts of persons within their positions. "A job description is a written record of the duties, responsibilities, and requirements of a particular job. It is concerned with the job itself and not with the worker. It should be recognized for what it is — a description, a guide, and not an inflexible standard to be followed slavishly."

A job description therefore should be a guide which allows the member to exercise his or her gifts in the best possible way. To make a job description a timeless, legalistic and binding document is to miss the intent of what a job description is intended to be. Since this is true, job descriptions need to be updated so that the gifts of members can be exercised to their full potential.

What is a Job Description?

While there are slight differences in definitions, depending upon the speaker or writer, most personnel administrators recognize the job description as one of three tools in this area of personnel administration: a job analysis, a job description, or a job specification. A brief look at a few key definitions is in order. The word "job" is defined as assignment of work calling for a set of duties, responsibilities, and conditions that are different from those of other work assignments." Job analysis is a procedure used in collecting the data needed for writing the job description. A job description is a systematic outline of the information obtained from the job analysis. It describes the job title, the principle function, including the person to whom the employee is responsible.

Responsibilities include a description of the work performed, the skills or training required, and relationships with other jobs and personnel. A job description can be written before or after a staff member is employed. If written before, remember it is a guide for both the prospective employee and the supervisor. In either instance it is not a straitjacket. It is the broad parameter staked out around the particular job assignment.

Writing the Job Description

The best job descriptions are specific, definite and measurable. The job description relates dynamically and vitally to the entire plan, lead, organization, central concept. And as it has been said, "People do what we inspect not what we expect."

Suggested format:

Each job description should contain these components:

- Introduction
- Job title
- Date of description
- Job summary
- Job duties
- Organizational relationships
- Qualifications
- Training and development
- Evaluation (annually)

Sample format outline:

The position of _____ is established by authorization of the _____, the Pentecostal Church of God. The job summary, duties, organizational

Job (Position) Descriptions

relationships, qualifications, training and development shall be as set forth in this job description.

JOB TITLE:

DATE:

HE REPORTS TO:

JOB SUMMARY:

The job summary shows the end result this position exists to accomplish. It must be definitive, measurable and specific. It is the most difficult part of the description to write.

JOB DUTIES:

These are activities necessary for the accomplishment of the above mentioned end result. We come to duties only when we settle the end result. Then list activities necessary to accomplish the end result.

ORGANIZATIONAL RELATIONSHIPS:

Relationships extend in four directions—up, down, and sideways in both directions. Principle of TO and FOR—responsible to, shows his superiors, responsible for, shows subordinates.

QUALIFICATIONS:

These are for the performance of the work. This is what the person should ideally be and know in order to most effectively accomplish the job summary. It is not a matter of "Here is what we want done," but, "Where is the person that can best do it?"

TRAINING AND DEVELOPMENT:

In other words, if this person does not measure up fully to these qualifications, he needs self-development to better qualify. We speak here about skills and abilities—about learning to do the job he has to do.

Sample job description using the above mentioned format:

MESSENGER PUBLISHING HOUSE
PRODUCTION MANAGER OF MESSENGER PRINTING OPERATION
JOB DESCRIPTION

The position of Production Manager of the Messenger Printing Operation is established by authorization of the Executive Committee of the Pentecostal Church of God. The job summary, duties, organizational relationships, qualifications, training and development shall be as set forth in this job description.

Inasmuch as the present policy and procedural manual is brief in work duties, responsibilities, and relationships as well as privileges of the position, the following is submitted for a more effective work performance.

NOTE: A job description is very important. It helps us to know what our tasks are in the organization. It helps our superior to know what we are doing. It helps us to know what he expects of us and it lets people around us know what we are doing.

JOB TITLE:

Production Manager of Messenger Printing Operation.

Job (Position) Descriptions

DATE:
January, 1982.

HE REPORTS TO:
Personnel Supervisor or General Superintendent and to the Executive Committee upon request and shall work directly under the Personnel Supervisor and General Superintendent.

JOB SUMMARY:
The position of Production Manager is established to supervise the printing operation of Messenger Publishing House. Responsibility for producing a particular item begins when the copy and printing instructions are received. By means of the personnel and equipment, that item is produced according to specifications and either added to inventory for sales or delivered to the department or customer making the order. The Production Manager shall also be responsible to supervise the maintenance and custodial care of the printing facility.

JOB DUTIES:
It shall be the duty of the Production Manager to provide supervision in the areas of:
1. Job scheduling.
2. Quality control.
3. Employee records.
4. Inventory Control (Raw and Finished materialso.)
5. Plan related accounting and billing process.
6. Equipment operation and maintenance.
7. Maintenance, custodial care, a security of printing facility.
8. Sales and distribution.
9. And, shall be chairman of the production staff and coordinate all printing procedures through said staff. The weekly staff meeting shall pro-

vide occasion for consideration of job flow to insure overall efficiency in the printing plant.
10. He shall be a member of the Editorial Staff.
11. And, perform other duties as requested.

Records and reports. The Production Manager shall be responsible for furnishing regular, timely reports to the General Business Manager and Editorial Staff concerning job progress, cost analysis, and needs related to the printing operation. He shall establish and maintain a systematic program of equipment maintenance for all mechanical equipment within his area of supervision. Routine records of operation shall be kept. All purchases will be made by purchase order in keeping with procedures established in conference with the Business Manager who shall endorse all purchase orders.

Employee relations. The Production Manager shall be responsible for keeping such employee records as are required for purposes of insurance and safety. He shall keep a record of accumulated employee benefits, such as sick leave and vacation time, and shall keep work hours within the established limits unless specific clearance has been secured for extending work hours. He shall submit weekly payroll information to the General Accounting Office over his signature.

Employee relations shall be a vital part of the duties of the Production Manager. He shall seek to create a spirit of unity and cooperation. He shall furnish recommendations concerning merit raises for employees by the first of November each year for consideration by the Executive Committee.

Printing costs. The Production Manager shall be responsible for preparation of estimates of printing costs. Personnel of the printing plant will be

Job (Position) Descriptions

available to assist in making estimates both accurate and profitable. Procedures for estimates will be developed in cooperation with the Business Manager.

Building security. The Production Manager shall maintain close supervision of all keys issued for entrance to the printing facility. He shall be responsible for security in that facility assuring that all doors are properly locked except during regular work hours.

Salary. The Production Manager shall be paid an hourly rate. The normal work schedule is for a week of 40 hours. Overtime must have the prior authorization of the personnel supervisor.

ORGANIZATIONAL RELATIONSHIPS:

1. The Production Manager has as his immediate superior the General Business Manager. Questions relating to action or policy which are not covered by standing policy will be resolved in conference with the Business Manager.
2. All policy or production changes which would alter the assigned work of the Production Manager must be approved by the Business Manager and General Superintendent.
3. Production personnel shall be subordinate to the Production Manager. However, all personnel are subject to the personnel supervisor.

Prerogative. The Production Manager may:
1. Make recommendations regarding needed personnel through the production staff and recommend purchases to enhance production and building maintenance.
2. Make adjustments in work schedule to facilitate production.
3. Make recommendations to the Business Man-

Administrative Resource Manual

ager relative to the proposed annual budget.
The Production Manager may not:
1. Absent himself from his assigned work schedule without prior notification and approval from the personnel supervisor.
2. Create any liability by signing a contract without expressed approval of the responsible officer.
3. Hire or terminate any employee (only by direction of responsible officer).

QUALIFICATIONS:
1. The Production Manager must be a born again Christian and living a consistent Christian life.
2. He must be experienced in the field of printing with knowledge of processes and equipment used.
3. Must be able to work with schedules and deadlines, communicate with his employees, and coordinate the work of his division through paid staff.
4. Should have prior knowledge of the objectives of the organization.
5. Shall be competent in management of people, time and schedules to accomplish the goals of production.

TRAINING AND DEVELOPMENT:
In order to improve skills and keep abreast of developments in the printing and management field and to develop an instrument describing policies and procedures not covered in the manual, the following shall apply:
1. A working guideline file shall be developed and kept at the desk as a resource on policy and procedure.
2. Attendance at all regular staff meetings.

Job (Position) Descriptions

3. Attendance at seminars and workshops relating to the task of the manager, by prior approval.
4. Researching of materials available, perhaps attendance to occasional classes, and perhaps representation in a membership association could be provided.

FINALLY:

It is understood that any job description will need review and possible updating annually. This is approved by the Executive Committee, January 5, 1982.

With this information given and the suggested format you should write a job description for every position that reports to a superior, board or convention body. It is suggested that each district organize an office working policy manual containing a clear job description for each position, along with other office guidelines needed for operation and effective administration.

Note: Messenger Publishing House markets a Church Office Administration kit on CD-ROM with abundant resources for church use (Item # 010153). For information, you may call:
(800) 444-4674.

CHAPTER 26
Communications

The developing of an effective communications network is vital to continued growth and progress on all levels of work.

One of the immediate needs in our church structure for effectively reaching our purpose is a viable communications system. The lack of good communications between the General, district and local levels of operation has contributed to our low growth performance, as we observed in the study committee on Evaluation of Structure.

To communicate is, "to give or exchange information by signals, messages, talk, gestures or writing." It is sending and receiving messages of information so that we may mutually understand and reach toward the same purpose, the transmitting of messages by any form—the art of expressing ideas in speaking and writing.

When certain things do not happen as planned it is said, "There is a breakdown in communications"—and this is true in most cases. Just talking is not necessarily communication, for we only know

Communications

that we have communicated when we hear the individual resound the message they received from us.

It is said, "communication is depositing a part of yourself in another person."

"Strides of communication now permit us to talk with people around the globe, but cannot bridge the ever-widening gaps within our own families" (Gloria France).

So then, to communicate is to impart something to one another, so that it becomes common to giver and receiver.

The following comments are by Dr. Fuller, President of Fuller Communication Service in Harrisonburg, Virginia:

> Communication networks process information. Messages must get to the right people, in the right places, on time and in an understandable form. When networks break down, communication fails and there are serious consequences. As many as 90 percent of all business failures are a direct result of communication breakdowns.
>
> There are two kinds of communication networks. The formal network is established by the company as the official chain-of-command. This network tends to be predictable and permanent. A distinctive feature of the formal network is its hierarchical structure with established gate keepers to regulate the flow of messages.
>
> The unofficial network is informal and is usually called the grapevine. It tends to be a dynamic, constantly changing structure, and messages flow without regularity or predictability. Two surprising features of the grape-

vine are its unusual quickness because there are not gate keepers and its 80 percent accuracy rate.

Poor communication is a major cause of low morale. Employee turnover is often a result of communication breakdown. It produces a lack of united purpose to reach common goals.

Research indicates that we learn 11 percent from listening, 83 percent from seeing and 6 percent from tasting, smelling and feeling. This information implies that oral messages are minimally effective. The addition of visual elements, however, increases learning dramatically. Directions, instruction and similar messages should be supported by using appropriate pictures, graphs, diagrams and other visual media. Oral messages with visual supporting material will more than double our rate of remembering.

CHAPTER 27
Bits and Pieces

PURPOSES, GOALS AND OBJECTIVES

The management must first identify the purpose of the church, then state what the church hopes to accomplish (goals), and finally outline steps (objectives) toward the achievement of those goals. His focus will always be on objectives rather than obstacles.

The purpose states "Why." The goals state "What." The objectives state "Where," "When" and "How."

Catchy themes, mottoes and generalizations can never take the place of clear-cut objectives. Many good ideas fail because they have not been made specific and reachable by definite goals and objectives. Leaders often make the mistake of trying to motivate people with rallying calls which lack a statement of precise action. The people do not respond because they do not know what actions to take. The leader may say, "Let's do something," but unless he further defines what needs doing, achievements are doubtful.

The sighting of goals and objectives helps to identify the results to be accomplished through purposeful action. Mere activity without attention to purpose seldom produces desirable ends. The trend is to lose sight of goals and have only activities. Churches generally have a clear concept of purpose in their beginning days. However, with the passing of time, the increasing preoccupation with activities, the erosion of the world, the death or moving away of original members, or spiritual decline, the church's emphasis tends to shift from specific goals to maintenance operations. A church is in decline when it finds pleasure only in the routine operations.

Objectives must be definitive so as to set boundaries; they must be measurable with quantitative values. They deal with how many, how big and when. These serve as bench marks to measure the church's progress in its mission for Christ.

Goals and objectives need to be reasonable and within the ability of the group to achieve. They need to be demanding enough to inspire the church to do its best. Motivation is inherent in challenging goals.

Goals become personalized by involving the entire group in their formation. This is accomplished when the pastor involves the church board and other committees in setting the goals.

Bennington Model

Another model for planning and administration is called the Bennington Model. It consists of four basic steps:

1. Vision
2. Mission
3. Plan
4. Action Steps

Vision

Vision is the guiding God-given direction for an entity. The vision should be put in a brief statement which encompasses what the leader believes to be God's overall direction and plan for the body. The Word teaches "Write the vision, and make it plan upon tables, that he may run that readeth it" (Habakkuk 2:2). A leader's vision must be in a form in which it may be freely and consistently communicated.

Mission

While there are similarities between the vision and mission, the mission in fact grows out of the vision. A mission statement is more concrete and defines specifically where the ministry is going.

Plan

Effective leaders know the advantage of a long-range plan. Once the vision and mission statements have been prepared, the next step is to develop a long-range plan, the most common one being a five-year plan. This plan is then broken down into annual plans. To be effective, a plan must include not only goals but methods for attaining those goals and difficulties which must be overcome to succeed. The five-year plan is revised each year to adjust to experience but is kept before all who are involved in carrying out the plan.

Action Steps

No plan is complete until it includes the day-to-day and week-to-week actions which will bring the plan to fulfillment. Only when the plan is brought to this level is it truly an effective plan.

The Word clearly demonstrates that God births in His chosen leaders a commission. With prayer and meditation this commission will result in a clearly-drawn vision out of which the entire process of effective leadership flows.

When a leader has prayerfully developed the vision and mission statements, these should become the guiding force controlling all decisions. Effective leaders are examining every aspect of administration to find those activities which are contrary to or not directly advancing the vision. This includes looking at how much of the time we spend in meetings dealing with the past (which we can't change) contrasted with the amount spent casting the vision into the hearts of other leaders and team members.

One suggestion growing out of the Bennington plan is that every meeting should be opened with the mission statement. Minutes (which only deal with the past) may well be left to the end of the meeting. A timed agenda will assure that the amount of time given to any item on the agenda reflects the vision and means of accomplishing God's plan. Our guiding philosophy should not be driven by the way things have been done but by how they should be done for accomplishing God's will.

CHAPTER 28
Sources and Resources

It has been said that the average person is about 10% original. This means that to succeed in life and in our tasks we will need a lot of resources. We are a resource to one another. Life is a learning experience. And thank God for those who have published their knowledge and data on life from their knowledge bank (the mind) in written form.

The following bibliography includes resources which may be helpful. Each is listed under subject title.

ADMINISTRATION/MANAGEMENT

Andrews, Sherry, et. al. *Solving the Ministry's Toughest Problems.* Strong Communications Company.

Bush, Myron. *Management: A Biblical Approach.* Victor Books.

Carnahan, Roy E. *Creative Pastoral Management.* Beacon Hill Press.

Drucker, Peter F. *The Effective Executive.* Harper & Row.

Eims, Leroy. *Be a Motivational Leader.* Victor Books.

Engstrom, Ted W. and Edward R. Dayton. *The Art of Management for Christian Leaders.* Word Publications.

— -. *The Christian Executive.* Word Publications.

Engstrom, Ted W. *Your Gift of Administration.* Thomas Nelson Publishers.

Fallon, William K. *AMA Management Handbook.* Amacom.

Hendrix, Olan. *Management for the Christian Worker.* Quill Publications.

Powers, Bruce P. *Christian Leadership.* Broadman Press.

CHURCH - MISSION/GROWTH

Barnett, Tommy; *Multiplication.* Creative House

Benjamine, Paul. *The Equipping Ministry.* Standard Publishing.

Hodges, Melvin L. *A Theology of the Church and Its Mission.* Gospel Publishing House.

LeTourneau, Richard. *Management Plus.* Zondervan Press.

McDonough, Reginald M. *A Church on a Mission.* Convention Press.

McGavran, Donald A. and Win Am. *How to Grow Your Church.* Regal.

Schuller, Robert H. *Your Church Has Real Possibilities.* Regal.

Wagner, C. Peter. *Your Church Can Grow.* Regal.

Warren, Rick. *The Purpose Driven Church.* Zondervan Publishing House.

Wilson, Aaron M. *My Church Can Grow.* Messenger Publishing House.

Bibliography

LEADERSHIP

Amerding, Hudson T. *Leadership.* Tyndale.

Engstrom, Ted W. The *Making of a Christian Leader.* Zondervan.

Getz, Gene A. *Sharpening the Focus of the Church.* Moody Press.

McDonough, Reginald M. *Growing Ministers, Growing Churches.* Convention Press.

Maxwell, John C. *Developing the Leaders Around You.* Thomas Nelson

__. *Developing the Leader Within You.* Thomas Nelson

__. *21 Irrefutable Laws of Leadership.* Thomas Nelson

Redpath, Alan. *The Making of a Man of God.* Revell.

Richards, Lawrence O. and Clyde Hoeldtke. *A Theology of Church Leadership.* Zondervan.

Sanders, J. Oswald. *Spiritual Leadership.* Moody Press.

Stoppe, Richard L. *Leadership Communication.* Pathway Press.

Swindoll, Charles R. *Hand Me Another Brick.* Thomas Nelson Publishing.

Zimmerman, T. F. *And He Gave Pastors.* Gospel Publishing House.

STEWARDSHIP

Brazell, George. *This Is Stewardship.* Gospel Publishing House.

Fooshe, George Jr. *You Can Be Financially Free.* Revell.

Knudsen, Raymond B. *New Models for Financing the Local Church.* Association Press.

Ralston, Holmes. *Stewardship in the New Testament Church.* John Knox Press.

Rein, R. C. *Adventures in Christian Stewardship.*

Administrative Resource Manual

Concordia Publishing House.

Young, Samuel. *Giving and Living*. Baker Book House.

Wilson, Aaron M. *Studies on Stewardship*. Messenger Publishing House.

DISCIPLESHIP

Bruce, A. B. *The Training of the Twelve*. Kregel Publications.

Coleman, Robert E. *The Master Plan of Evangelism*. Revell.

— -. *The Mind of the Master*. Revell.

HELPS

Cairnes, Earle E. *Christianity Through the Centuries*. Zondervan.

Dayton, Edward R. *Tools for Time Management*. Zondervan.

Hammar, Richard R. *Pastor, Church and Law*. Gospel Publishing House.

Rush, Myron D. *Richer Relationships*. Victor Books.

Strong, Augustus H. *Systematic Theology*. Revell.

Eims, Leroy. *The Lost Art of Disciple Making*. Zondervan/NavPress.

Henrichsen, Walter A. *Disciples Are Made Not Born*. Victor Books.

Sheets, Dutch. *Intercessory Prayer*. Regal Books.

Thiessen, Henry Clarence. *Lectures on Systematic Theology*. Erdman Publishing.

Williams, Elizabeth. *Prevision of History*. Messenger Publishing House.

___. *The International Standard Bible Encyclopedia*. Erdman Publishing.

___. *Ordination*. Gospel Publishing House.

Bibliography

PENTECOST: HOLY SPIRIT

Brumback, Carl. *What Meaneth This.* Gospel Publishing House.

Carlson, G. Raymond. *The Acts Story.* Gospel Publishing House.

—-. *Spiritual Dynamics.* Gospel Publishing House.

Horton, Stanley M. *What the Bible Says About the Holy Spirit.* Gospel Publishing House.

Incidentally, *the Bible sheds a lot of light on these books!*